PEARL
IN ITS SETTING

PEARL

IN ITS SETTING

A Critical Study of the Structure and
Meaning of the Middle English Poem

By IAN BISHOP
Lecturer in English
University of Bristol

BASIL BLACKWELL
OXFORD
1968

© Basil Blackwell, 1968

631 11410 6

*Library of Congress Catalog
Card Number 68 – 28309*

PRINTED IN GREAT BRITAIN
BY ROBERT CUNNINGHAM AND SONS LTD, ALVA

Contents

PART THREE

SOURCES FOR THE CHARACTERIZATION
OF THE MAIDEN

Acknowledgements

My first, tentative inquiries into the structure and meaning of *Pearl* were undertaken some years ago as part of the work for the Oxford B.Litt. degree. This work was begun under the supervision of the Rev. Gervase Mathew and completed under that of Professor J. R. R. Tolkien. To both of these scholars I am indebted for their great kindness and encouragement at that time; had it not been for the interest which they took in my work then, the present study would probably never have been begun. My chief debt is to Professor J. A. W. Bennett who encouraged and guided my undergraduate studies of medieval literature and has always taken a kindly interest in my work on *Pearl*. After reading the present monograph in typescript, he offered valuable advice and helpful criticism from which I have tried to profit. It is also a pleasure to record with thanks the painstaking help and scrupulous advice that I have received from Dr Basil Cottle, who generously transferred his attention from the far more congenial and worthwhile task of completing a book of his own in order to read the proofs of this one. All particular debts are recorded, to the best of my knowledge, at the appropriate place in the notes. My thanks are also due to Mr and Mrs John Farrell for compiling the index; to both my mother and my father for assistance of various kinds in the preparation of this book; to the Trustees of the Colston Research Society of Bristol for a substantial grant to cover secretarial expenses; and to the Delegates of the Clarendon Press for permission to quote from the text and *apparatus* of E. V. Gordon's edition of *Pearl* and for allowing me to reproduce – with modifications – three paragraphs of an article of mine that appeared in *The Review of English Studies* in February 1957.

I.B.B.

Bristol,
August 1968

Abbreviations

Anal. Hymnica	Dreves, Guido Maria, and Clemens Blume, edd., *Analecta Hymnica Medii Aevi* (Leipzig, 1886–)
CSEL	*Corpus Scriptorum Ecclesiasticorum Latinorum*
EETS	*Early English Text Society* (O.S. = Original Series; E.S. = Extra Series)
JEGP	*Journal of English and Germanic Philology*
M. AE.	*Medium Aevum*
MED	*Middle English Dictionary*, ed. H. Kurath and S. M. Kuhn; S. M. Kuhn and J. Reidy
MHRA	Modern Humanities Research Association
MLN	*Modern Language Notes*
MP	*Modern Philology*
OED	*Oxford English Dictionary*
PG	J.-P. Migne (ed.), *Patrologia Graeca*
PL	J.-P. Migne (ed.), *Patrologia Latina*
PMLA	*Publications of the Modern Language Association of America*
RES	*Review of English Studies* (N.S. = New Series)
SATF	Société des Anciens Textes Français
SP	*Studies in Philology*
ST	St. Thomas Aquinas, *Summa Theologiae*

Introduction

(i) *Pearl* AND ITS SETTING

A decade ago I published an article on 'The Significance of the "Garlande Gay" in the Allegory of *Pearl*',[1] in which I discussed, among other things, the importance in the poem's argument of the theme of the ideal setting for the pearl. I indicated how at the beginning of the poem the ideal setting for the gem is declared to be 'in golde so clere', but that by the time we reach ll. 22–24 we find the narrator lamenting the fact that his pearl is now encased in a far from ideal setting; for it is clothed in clods of earth. In his vision, however, he is first reassured that the pearl is in fact preserved in the treasure-chest of the heavenly paradise and eventually he sees her restored to a setting of gold and light in the New Jerusalem.

In the present study I attempt to do for the poem itself something similar to what is done for the pearl in the course of the development of that particular 'conceit'. At the time of its composition the beauty and the meaning of the poem must have shone out much more clearly than they do today, enhanced as they were by being set in literary, intellectual, cultural and ecclesiastical traditions that would have been perfectly familiar to its educated readers or audience. During the five succeeding centuries, when it remained buried and unknown to the literary public, its clarity became obscured by accumulated layers of ignorance as educated men gradually lost touch with several of those traditions of thought and feeling that were crystallized in its original composition. Since Richard Morris's edition of the MS. for the Early English Text Society in 1864 rescued the poem from oblivion, many other scholars have – with varying degrees of success – assisted in the attempt to restore its original brightness. With the publication in 1953 of E. V. Gordon's valuable edition,[2] *Pearl* was indeed provided with a worthy 'forser' and all later students of the poem must be grateful to Professor and Mrs Gordon – and the other scholars upon whose work they draw – that it is now 'in cofer so comly clente'.

Nevertheless, it seems to me that much work still remains to be done before *Pearl* can be displayed once more shining with its original clarity in its proper setting. It is particularly important for us to try to reconstruct the original 'setting' because a knowledge of those largely forgotten intellectual and cultural traditions out of which the poem grew can considerably increase our understanding of it. Perhaps an even more important reason for making the attempt is the merely negative one that the recovery of such knowledge may prevent us from misinterpreting both the poem's *sensus* and its *sententia*.

Before I describe in more detail what these traditions are, it must be emphasized that the recovery of such knowledge is no substitute for interpretation and criticism. Even to its original readers *Pearl* cannot have seemed the easiest of poems to appreciate. Its style is often elliptical; its thought sometimes elusive; its use of allegory and symbolism subtle; its structure complex. Throughout the course of this study I shall be concerned with such intrinsic difficulties of interpretation and with making a critical appraisal of the poet's achievement. But most of my space will inevitably be taken up with exhibiting the relevant historical material and with the application of it to the interpretation of the poem.

An extraordinary wealth of material is concentrated within the comparatively narrow compass of *Pearl*. No less remarkable is the variety of unsuspected places from which may be gathered external evidence that is capable of illuminating the poem's meaning and its structure. In the article to which I have already referred I suggested that a solution to a particular crux in the text could be found in such an unlikely place as the inscriptions on certain ecclesiastical candelabra. In the following pages I hope to bring out the full significance of a number of other details in the text, but I shall be mainly concerned with broader and more fundamental questions. One of these is the question of the poem's literary *genre*. Until quite recently most students of *Pearl* were unaware of the very existence of the peculiar *genre* to which it belongs. In attempting to assign it wrongly to another *genre* – the elegy – they often misunderstood the author's intention and, at the same time, laid themselves open to attack from those who, aware that the poem could not be satisfactorily explained as an elegy, maintained that it must be interpreted as total allegory. Even the scholars who have assigned it to what seems to me to be its proper *genre* appear to have a very limited knowledge of that *genre* and do not realize the full implications that the attribution has for an understanding of the poem. This question of *genre* affords a clear example of the need to study the poem in its 'setting': in Chapter One I shall examine the characteristics of the *genre* and demonstrate how a knowledge of this subject can enhance our understanding of *Pearl*.

Two other aspects of the poem that seem to me to have received insufficient attention are its structure and the purpose and conduct of the debate between the dreamer and the maiden. A careful, internal examination of the text itself will yield most of what needs to be observed about these two aspects. Nevertheless, external, historical knowledge again provides a lamp that can facilitate the examination. Medieval principles and ideals of literary structure differed in some important respects from those to which the modern reader is accustomed: some knowledge of these principles will certainly enable us better to appreciate the curious structure of *Pearl*. Similarly, the conduct of the debate can be more readily understood if we know something about the rules and the techniques of the medieval *disputatio*.

Having discussed in Part One its plan and purpose, I arrive in Part Two at what is usually the first aspect of the poem to be considered by those who have offered interpretations of *Pearl*; indeed, all too often it is the only aspect which they consider. I mean the author's use of allegory and symbolism. Its importance is suggested by the amount that has been written about it; yet I believe that it is still not properly understood. Gordon's remarks on the subject are eminently sensible: they indicate that a number of earlier interpretations went astray because their authors' presuppositions about medieval allegory were oversimplified.[3] But even Gordon seems to me not to realize how complex the subject is and not to recognize completely just how subtle and profound is the poet's use of allegorical thought and expression. Indeed, it would appear that the knowledge and understanding of medieval allegory possessed by many students of Middle English literature is somewhat limited – whether they are concerned with *Pearl*, *Piers Plowman* or the 'dream allegories' of Chaucer. It therefore seems to me necessary to make a fairly radical investigation of this subject; especially as *Pearl* is, from this point of view, the most complex of all Middle English poems. Such an investigation must increase by a certain amount the length of my inquiry, but it also endows it with what may be considered a compensating advantage: the scope of this study is thereby broadened so that it may offer something not only to students of *Pearl*, but also to anyone who is interested in the use of allegory and symbolism in medieval literature generally. So the reader who opens this volume mainly out of curiosity to see what yet another interpretation of *Pearl* can possibly have to say will perhaps be well advised to omit – at a first reading – the first section of Chapter Four and the whole of Chapter Five. However, I trust that, if he does so, he will refrain from dismissing as arbitrary and unhistorical my interpretation of the poem, contained in the final section of Chapter Four and throughout the whole of Chapter Six, before he has read the sections that he had omitted.

To devote three chapters to a study of sources for the characterization of the maiden may seem excessive – especially to those readers who would maintain that she is not characterized at all, but is merely a mouthpiece for the presentation of doctrinal matter. But long before I reach Part Three I shall argue that she is more than that; later I shall show that considerable knowledge and imaginative skill were needed by a poet who wished to provide an authentic and convincing representation of a particular heavenly being. The sources to which I shall refer in Part Three are twofold: medieval poetic tradition, and liturgical texts and commentaries. The poetic traditions have been discussed often enough; our poet's peculiar use of them has not. The only scholar to have made use of the liturgy to illuminate an important detail of the presentation of the maiden is Elizabeth Hart.[4] I shall argue that a knowledge of medieval liturgical texts and commentaries will not only explain many other details of the characterization of the maiden, but may also help to confirm the interpretation of the poem as a whole which is developed in the two earlier parts of this monograph.

I do not claim to have done more than restore a part of the

poem's original setting. Other scholars will be able to show how other medieval texts and traditions of thought may help us to a fuller understanding of *Pearl*. Moreover, I have avoided any discussion of certain major texts that could have been used to support my interpretation: for example, the whole corpus of exegetical, psychological and mystical treatises by the great Cistercians and Victorines. I have preferred to concentrate for the most part upon analogues and sources that are likely to have been accessible to the educated layman of the fourteenth century rather than those that were intended for the advanced specialist in the contemplative life.[5]

(ii) THE OCCASION OF THE POEM'S COMPOSITION

Before I offer any new suggestions about the meaning and structure of *Pearl* I must declare, as unequivocally as possible, the position that I adopt in the controversy that has preoccupied many students of the poem during the present century, concerning the occasion of its composition. Most scholars believe that this occasion was the death of a child, presumably the poet's daughter, before she was two years old. In the poem the dead child is represented as appearing to the narrator in a vision in which she assures him that she now enjoys eternal life in the Kingdom of Heaven. That is what the poem purports to be about, so it is hardly surprising that most scholars have accepted this view; among them is Gordon, who defends it with admirable good sense in the introduction to his edition.[6] Those who have denied this personal interpretation have mounted their attack mainly from two directions. First, they argue that there is insufficient evidence in the text to warrant any confident assertion that the maiden was the poet's daughter. Their other contention is that *Pearl* undoubtedly contains elements of allegory and symbolism: is it not probable, therefore, that the maiden herself is nothing more than a symbol of some abstract quality and her premature death merely an allegory of some purely spiritual occurrence? The shortest reply to these objections is that all the attempts that have so far been made to maintain such a totally allegorical view of the poem involve many more difficulties, inconsistencies and illogical deductions than have appeared in attempts to defend the personal interpretation.[7]

Nevertheless, the difficulties involved in the personal interpretation are perhaps a little more formidable than Gordon is willing to admit and it would be disingenuous of me to pass silently over them. I shall examine the question of allegory and symbolism in Part Two, but it is possible to say at this stage that Gordon's condemnation of these interpretations that regard the poem as total allegory seems to me to be substantially justified. The totally allegorical approach claims that the whole poem is something other than what it purports to be: it regards it as a full-length mantle of fiction that is designed to cover some deliberately hidden truth. But there is another sense in which the poem could be regarded as something other than what it purports to be, without resorting to allegory: it may be primarily a theological debate that is placed in a feigned autobiographical setting in order to make the 'doctrine' more palatable and the issues debated more urgent. Gordon has envisaged this possibility too and has provided a sufficient answer to those who would support it.[8]

The particular problem that is to be discussed now does not concern the historicity of the autobiographical elements in the poem so much as the verisimilitude of their presentation. Supporters of the personal interpretation must be prepared to admit quite openly that much of the biographical material is presented in a somewhat elusive manner and some of it even in a cryptic, allegorical disguise.

In the opening stanzas the child's death is referred to obscurely under a cloak of allegory and even the non-allegorical details of the mourner's visit to her graveplot offend against the canons of verisimilitude, as we shall see later.[9] But I shall also argue later that the author has a particular reason for presenting the situation in such a way at this point.[10] During the account of the vision some fairly plain facts about the child's biography are stated; but they are revealed to the reader only sporadically as the action of the 'plot' requires.[11] Apart from statements that merely help us to identify the vision-maiden as the soul of the dead child, the two most important facts to be disclosed are: (a) that she lived for less than two years 'in oure þede' and so had learnt not even the rudiments of religious instruction (ll. 483–85); (b) that 'Ho watz me nerre þen aunte or nece' (l. 233). The slight imprecision of the statement about the

child's age is probably deliberate: the poet has special reasons
for wishing to associate the maiden with the Holy Innocents –
the children 'a bimatu et infra' whom Herod ordered to be
slain.[12] The teasingly incomplete disclosure of the nature of her
relationship to the mourner is probably due to the poet's desire
to enable the reader to share with the dreamer the experience
of recognizing only gradually the maiden whom he sees 'in so
straunge a place' and so strangely transfigured. Like the
ἀναγνώρισις in classical drama, this recognition scene is long
drawn out – there are over seventy lines between the one in
which the dreamer first catches sight of the 'faunt' and that in
which this vague statement of kinship is vouchsafed us – and
proceeds by means of hints rather than clear statements of fact.
So the obscurity which the modern reader finds in this instance
actually arises from the author's wish to achieve verisimilitude
in the presentation of the vision. The fact that he could afford
to adopt such an allusive method suggests that his original
readers, or audience, knew perfectly well what the exact
relationship between the child and her mourner was. The
author's failure to state the precise relationship may therefore
be adduced as evidence that the autobiographical elements in
the poem are historical – though it is dangerous to set too much
store by negative evidence.

The confusion that this partial reticence causes the modern
reader does not by itself amount to very much, but it is aggra-
vated by an instance of complete reticence whose importance
Gordon appears to have underestimated. The recognition scene
reaches its climax when the dreamer engages the maiden
in conversation and immediately puts to her the question of
her identity, which has been teasing him throughout the
episode:

> ' "O Perle", quod I, "in perleȝ pyȝt,
> Art þou my perle þat I haf playned,
> Regretted by myn one on nyȝte?" '   (ll. 241–43)

Line 243 makes us acutely aware of the fact that the child's
mother is never mentioned in the poem. Various attempts have
been made to account for the author's reticence on this point,
including the suggestion that she was unfaithful or that the
child was illegitimate. But the simplest explanation would

appear to be that the mother died in childbirth, or soon after. The surviving child would thus have become particularly precious to its father and a comfort to him. Indeed, the narrator says of the lost infant that she

> '. . . wont watȝ whyle deuoyde my wrange
> And heuen my happe and al my hele.'   (ll. 15–16)

When the child, in turn, was snatched away from him it may well have seemed to him that some malicious and merciless power was in control of human affairs, and so he was cast down into the depths of despair.

But even if we assume this hypothesis to be correct, the poet's reticence about the mother may still seem surprising: we might have expected him to have erected in verse a double monument to his wife and child. It is here that the question of the poem's *genre* becomes relevant. In Chapter One I shall argue that *Pearl* is not in essence a memorial to the deceased infant; it is rather an account of how, as a result of meditating upon her premature death, the narrator received spiritual illumination and benefit. The poem's peculiar moral and spiritual *sentence* is derived from the fact that it is specifically upon the figure of the child that the mourner meditates. The mother is, in truth, irrelevant to the essential theme of the poem.

In the absence of any external evidence, we must be prepared for the possibility that this assumption about the mother's death is mistaken – though it would seem to be the simplest and most natural hypothesis to make about the situation that is presented in the poem. Nevertheless, I believe that it would not be impossible to account for the poet's reticence and yet to 'salve the appearances' in the text, even if it is assumed that the mourner's wife remained alive and faithful and that she was indeed the child's mother. Similarly, the hypothesis about the relationship between mourner and child may be incorrect: she may have been a god-child, a grand-child or even a younger sister. But Professor Norman Davis[13] has recently added another interesting piece of evidence to Gordon's cogent arguments[14] for assuming that she was the mourner's own daughter. Perhaps the most impressive of Gordon's arguments in support of this particular point is one that stands quite independently of any surmise about the author's biography:

'The depth of sorrow portrayed for a child so young belongs rather to parenthood. And there seems to be a special significance in the situation where the doctrinal lesson given by the celestial maiden comes from one of no earthly wisdom to her proper teacher and instructor in the natural order.'[15]

PART ONE

GENRE AND STRUCTURE

CHAPTER ONE

Genre

In the course of the panegyric of the pearl, with which the poem
begins, the narrator remarks:

> 'Quere-so-euer I jugged gemmeȝ gaye,
> I sette hyr sengeley in synglere.'

One of the purposes of the present study is to set the poem
itself 'sengeley in synglere', apart from all other literary
compositions, by demonstrating its uniqueness. To begin my
study with speculation about its *genre* may seem inconsistent
with this purpose. The pedantic pastime of assigning works to ·
particular *genres* often produces criticism that is the opposite of
discriminating; it can reduce vital and individual works of
imaginative literature to a dead level of monotony and con-
formity. Nevertheless, recognition of the fact that a work belongs
to a particular *genre*, though dangerous when treated as a means
of establishing a paradigm for criticism of that work, may help
us by indicating at least the direction in which we should
proceed for an understanding of the author's intention.

But how is the *genre* of *Pearl* to be determined? Can it indeed
be assigned to a single *genre*? It appears to embrace several: its
use of an elaborate stanzaic structure may suggest a lyrical
mode, but its dominant mode is, in fact, narrative; its central
sections employ the semi-dramatic mode of dialogue, and this
dialogue has many of the features of the verse debate – a
recognized literary type in the Middle Ages. Some minor
genres also are present. The narrative contains two protracted
descriptions – description had been elevated almost to the status
of a *genre* ever since the authors of the twelfth-century *Artes
Poeticae* commended it as their favourite method of 'amplifica-
tion'. In the course of the debate occurs a free rendering of the

parable of the labourers in the vineyard, an instance of the very popular, ancillary narrative *genre* known as *exemplum*. The poem ends quite properly with a prayer, but begins with an adaptation of one of the most curious literary *genres* ever devised: the verse Lapidary.

As the narrative is mainly an account of a vision, and since poems about dreams constituted a popular literary type in the later Middle Ages, it might be thought that this is the all-embracing *genre* to which the others I have mentioned are subordinated. Certainly a comparison of *Pearl* with other poems of this type is illuminating; especially when it is compared with those in which the narrator's waking experiences are recorded as well as his dream. The relationship between the dream and the waking experience that precedes it is almost as intriguing in this poem as it is in *The Book of the Duchess* and *The Parlement of Foules*. The poet's handling of the dream suggests that he had a good knowledge of medieval theories of dream psychology and that he used this scientific knowledge in a manner comparable in sensitivity and imaginativeness with that of Chaucer in his 'love visions'. There is no need for me to examine this aspect of his work in detail because it has recently been treated very perceptively by Constance Hieatt.[1]

To describe *Pearl* as a 'dream-vision', however, does not tell us much about its plan or purpose. The *Roman de la Rose* and *Piers Plowman* both belong to this category, but the two poems are quite different in their plan and purpose. The two love-visions of Chaucer that have just been mentioned, even though somewhat alike in plan, are completely different kinds of poem: *The Book of the Duchess* is an elegy that has as its occasion the death of a real woman; *The Parlement of Foules* is a poetic exploration – probably not inspired by any historical occasion – of differing attitudes towards earthly love and of its place in the scheme of things. The distinctive feature of *The Book of the Duchess* is its elegiac purpose; it uses the fiction of a dream as its mode of expression. *Pearl* has often been compared in this respect with Chaucer's poem, but it has long been recognized that a closer parallel is afforded by Boccaccio's Eclogue XIV, 'Olympia'.[2] Under the guise of a classical pastoral, Boccaccio's poem is concerned, like *Pearl*, with a vision (though not in the course of a feigned dream) of the beatified soul of the deceased

herself – in this instance the poet's daughter, Violante, who had
died at the age of five and a half.

The continuing controversy about the *genre* of *Pearl* has not,
however, been concerned with the question of whether the poem
should be described as an Elegy or a Vision, but whether it is an
Elegy or an Allegory. The autobiographical interpretation of
Pearl was challenged as long ago as 1904 by W. H. Schofield[3]
and ever since then there has been a debate between those –
including E. V. Gordon – who regard it is an elegy and those
who, following Schofield's lead, believe it to be basically an
allegory.[4] The main reasons for supposing it to be an allegory
are the use of the pearl as a symbol and the presence in the
poem of a considerable amount of doctrinal and theological
material that might seem out of place in an elegy. Most modern
readers will probably accept Gordon's view, discussed in my
introductory chapter, that the poem has a personal bereavement as its occasion and that it cannot be regarded as an
example of 'total allegory'. However, it does not follow that, if
one accepts this view, one must also accept the term 'elegy' as
the most appropriate designation.

Dorothy Everett[5] argues that, although *Pearl* contains both
elegiac and allegorical elements, 'it is not to be comprehended
by either term'. She continues:

> '. . . it could with as much justice be called a homily, a
> debate (*disputatio*), or a vision of the other world. None of
> these labels, by itself, is any more illuminating than the
> bare terms "elegy" or "pastoral" would be, if applied to
> *Lycidas*.'[6]

However, in spite of the presence of its doctrinal and admoni-
tory elements, *Lycidas* fulfils the customary functions of an elegy
in a way that *Pearl* does not: it is primarily a lament for the
deceased and a monument erected in his honour. *Pearl* is concerned rather with consoling the bereaved than with mourning
the deceased. It is true that an element of consolation is often
present in an elegy, but in *Pearl* consolation is the fundamental
purpose that unifies the argument and determines its direction.
In the opening stanzas the mourner is discovered in a state of
rebellious and despairing grief, but by the end of the poem he
has arrived at a state of resignation to the Divine Will and

reached a mood of assurance and hope. The transition is effected by means of the vision in which the maiden assures him that she is saved and indicates to him the way in which he can himself obtain salvation.

It is therefore interesting to observe that from the time of the Greek writer Crantor (c. 335–c. 275 B.C.) Consolation was recognized as a literary *genre* in its own right.[7] Among classical Latin authors who made important contributions to the *genre* of the *consolatio mortis* were Cicero and Seneca. The principal custom of the *genre* was the citation of *solacia, loci communes* or 'topics' of consolation, which were handed down from one generation of practitioners to another. Early Christian writers adapted many of the pagan *solacia* to accord with their own beliefs and added new ones of their own. Such *solacia* are to be found in English literature from the earliest times: Professor J. E. Cross has identified a number of them in the Old English 'elegy', *The Wanderer*, and refers to examples in Chaucer.[8] Two other scholars have associated *Pearl* itself with the *genre*.

The first of these is John Conley in a paper on '*Pearl* and a Lost Tradition'[9] – the lost tradition being that of the Christian consolation. Unfortunately the only work with which he makes a detailed comparison of the poem is Boethius's *De Consolatione Philosophiae*, which is not a *consolatio mortis*, but offers more general consolation against the blows of Fortune. Nevertheless the article is valuable in so far as it brings out the importance of the Boethian concept of the *summum bonum* for an understanding of *Pearl*.[10]

Much nearer the mark is a paper by V. E. Watts,[11] which compares *Pearl* with some Christian consolations of the fourth century – all of them examples of the *consolatio mortis*. In particular, Mr Watts compares our poem with *Carmen* xxxi of Paulinus of Nola,[12] which offers consolation to Pneumatius and his wife Fidelis on the loss of their son Celsus, who had died before his eighth birthday.[13] At the end of this poem the child is associated with the company of *virgines* who follow the Lamb. Another respect in which it resembles *Pearl* is in its inclusion of a considerable amount of doctrinal and theological material. As in several of the other *consolationes* of the fourth century, the doctrinal material comprises a very long digression whose relevance to the consolatory purpose is not always apparent.

But Paulinus's poem comes even closer to *Pearl* than Mr Watts supposes. The poet is personally involved in the loss which it mourns: the death of the son of Pneumatius reminds him of that of his own son (also called Celsus) who had lived for only eight days. He imagines the two boys together in the company of the Holy Innocents. The relevant lines have been translated into English by no less distinguished a poet than Henry Vaughan:

> 'This pledge of your joint love, to Heaven now fled,
> With honey-combs and milk of life is fed.
> Or with the *Bethlem*-Babes (whom *Herods* rage
> Kill'd in their tender, happy, holy age)
> Doth walk the groves of Paradise, and make
> Garlands, which those young Martyrs from him take.
> With these his Eyes on the mild lamb are fixt,
> A Virgin-Child with Virgin-infants mixt.
> Such is my *Celsus* too, who soon as given,
> Was taken back (on the eighth day) to Heaven,
> To whom at *Alcala* I sadly gave
> Amongst the Martyrs Tombes a little grave.
> He now with yours (gone both the blessed way,)
> Amongst the trees of life doth smile and play;
> And this one drop of our mixt blood may be
> A light for my *Theresia*, and for me.'[14]

The only Christian *solacium* that Mr Watts cites is the hope of life after death. But *Pearl* in fact contains a considerable variety of these 'topics'. A careful examination of the way in which some of them are woven into the poet's argument will help us to perceive more clearly his purpose in writing the poem.

The most conspicuous example of a consolatory 'topic' in *Pearl* occurs in ll. 31–32:

> 'For vch gresse mot grow of grayneȝ dede;
> No whete were elleȝ to woneȝ wonne.'

This is based upon *John* xii, 24, and possibly I *Corinthians* xv, 34–38; it is the only explicit Biblical allusion in the introductory stanzas. However, it occurs so frequently, with reference to the resurrection of the dead, in Christian consolations that it must be accounted a commonplace of that *genre*. In her monograph on *Consolation in St. Augustine*[15] Sister Mary M. Beyenka remarks that the first writer of consolations to use this topic was Clement

of Rome (c. 30–100). She also cites examples from Gregory of
Nyssa[16]; Zeno of Verona (fourth century)[17]; Paulinus of Nola.[18]
Her example from the last of these is from his *Epistle* xiii.
Curiously enough, she does not mention his *Carmen* xxxi, the
poem about Celsus; but, in fact, the topic does occur there at
ll. 229 ff., along with other metaphors from Nature that were
regarded as consolatory 'topics'.[19] Most of her examples come,
as one would expect, from St. Augustine himself.[20] The most
elaborately developed example is in his *Sermo* 361[21]; it includes
a reference to the wheat's being gathered into the barn (cf.
Pearl l. 32).[22]

Three of the commonest of the ancient *solacia* adopted by
Christian writers are closely related topics: 'death is the common lot of man'; the necessity of submitting to Fate – or in
Christian times to the Will of God; 'nothing is to be gained by
immoderate grief'.[23] Professor Cross quotes from a consolatory
letter by the Emperor Julian (the Apostate) in which all three
are cited together.[24] It is interesting to see that Julian, employing the figure *occupatio*, refuses to invoke such arguments because
his correspondent would be all too familiar with them. The
first of these three topics is one of the oldest: in fact, Curtius[25]
gives an example from Homer as the earliest in a list of variations on this theme. It is perhaps the one consolatory 'topic' that
most English readers recognize as a commonplace, on account
of Gertrude's glib use of it in *Hamlet*, I, ii, 72 ff., its reiteration
by Justice Shallow, and Tennyson's rejection of it in the sixth
lyric of *In Memoriam*. This particular 'topic' is not used as a
consolatory argument in *Pearl* – unless the metaphor, in ll.
269–70, of the rose subject to the laws of Nature be regarded as a
variation of it. But the poet uses the other two 'topics' in close
conjunction. The opening stanzas contain a notable display of
grief, including the mourner's refusal of the consolations from
both Reason and 'kynde of Kryst' (l. 55).[26] The mourner's
tendency to despair is evident again at ll. 325 ff., after the
maiden has told him that he cannot satisfy immediately his
impulsive desire to cross the stream and be reunited with her.
The maiden's reply, contained in the two stanzas beginning with
l. 337, combines the themes of the unprofitability of contentious
grief and the benefits of submitting to God's Will; if one sub-
mits one may receive Divine consolation:

' "Hys comforte may þy langour lyþe
And þy lurez of lyztly fleme." '   (ll. 357–58)

Another 'topic' that occurs regularly in *consolationes* is 'life is a loan'.[27] Sister Beyenka notes that it is one of the Stoic commonplaces advanced by Seneca[28]; but the most interesting example for our present purpose is one that she quotes from a Consolatory Letter of Augustine to Probus:

> '. . . God, the Creator, has but taken away what He gave. He has willed to take back what had been bestowed for a brief while only. God has taken nothing of yours, when He took His own possession; He is like a creditor to whom only thanks are now due.'[29]

One is reminded of the stanza that reaches its climax with the maiden's rebuke:

' "And þou hatz called þy wyrde a þef
Þat ozt of nozt hatz made þe cler." '   (ll. 273–74)

We shall see later how the poet develops the argument that the child was never the mourner's property; he rejoices that she is now in the possession of her rightful owner, the Prince of Heaven.[30]

Two more topics are of particular importance for an understanding of the poem's argument and an appreciation of its purpose: they are the exhortation to the bereaved to imitate the virtues of the deceased; and the *solacium* of the *opportunitas mortis* – the argument that death occurred at the most opportune moment for the deceased and that it was indeed a positive advantage for him. The latter *solacium* is particularly appropriate when the deceased was snatched away in youth. The Stoics made the point that early death frees a man from many miseries; the Christian counterpart to this is that early death enables a man to avoid the risk of sins.[31] In his treatise *On The Early Death of Infants* Gregory of Nyssa argues that such a death is not a calamity, but an act of God's providence, because these children are saved from lives of evil.[32] A main argument in *Pearl* is that it was a positive advantage for the child to have died while still in a state of post-baptismal innocence; as an innocent she enters without question into Heaven. The dreamer

had maintained that she ought to receive an inferior reward to
that of the man

> ' "Þat endured in worlde stronge,
> And lyued in penaunce hys lyueȝ longe . . ." ' (ll. 476–77)

But the maiden replies:

> ' "Where wysteȝ þou euer any bourne abate,
> Euer so holy in hys prayere,
> Þat he ne forfeted by sumkyn gate
> Þe mede sumtyme of heueneȝ clere?
> *And ay þe ofter, þe alder þay were,*
> Þay laften ryȝt and wroȝten woghe." '
> $\qquad\qquad\qquad\qquad$ (ll. 617–22 – my italics)

In the argument of the poem this topic is associated with the
poet's development of the exhortation to imitate the virtues of
the deceased. This commonplace dates back to pagan antiquity,
but was adopted – with appropriate modifications – by Christians. Beyenka gives examples from Gregory of Nazianzus,
Sulpicius Severus and Augustine. The example from a consolatory letter by Sulpicius Severus on the death of Martin of
Tours argues that the deceased has gone ahead, showing the
way to Heaven by his virtues; he intercedes with God for his
friends.[33] It may be thought that this commonplace could not
occur in *Pearl*, because, although the child died before she
could commit sin (as we have just observed), her early death
also prevented her from performing any good deeds that could
be imitated. It is, therefore, interesting to find it used by
Paulinus of Nola at the conclusion of *Carmen* xxxi. After addressing Celsus, and his own child, and asking them to intercede for
their parents,[34] the poet urges the parents to imitate the
simplicitas of their children, if they wish to be reunited with
them in heaven.[35] Similarly, the author of *Pearl* argues that it is
perilous for a man to rely on his own righteousness; the only
certain hope is for him to recover the innocence that was
bestowed upon him by Grace at his baptism; the only way to
enter heaven is to become as a little child. Moreover, it is
obvious that the maiden has interceded with Christ on the
mourner's behalf – a fact which she states explicitly at ll. 966–
68:

' "Þou may not enter wythinne hys tor,
Bot of þe Lombe I haue þe aquylde
For a syȝt þerof þurȝ gret fauor." '

So this topic appears in *Pearl* in a somewhat unexpected form.
But enough has already been said to show that this is only one
of a number of individual transmutations that the poet effects
upon the well-used stock-in-trade of consolatory rhetoric. The
transformation of this particular topic also results in a further
development of the *opportunitas mortis* theme: the child's early
death comes to be regarded not only as a positive advantage for
her, but also as having spiritual benefits for the mourner himself.[36]

There can be no doubt, then, that *Pearl* contains a number of
examples of the consolatory commonplaces that were known in
pagan antiquity and were adapted by the Christian writers of
consolations in the fourth century. Their occurrence in the poem
may be nothing more than a coincidence. But that seems unlikely, and this impression is further substantiated as soon as we
look at some of the external evidence for the knowledge and use
of such 'topics' in the fourteenth century. Mr Watts has shown
that MSS. of some of the fourth-century consolations were
available in England during the fourteenth century.[37] I shall
now show that many of these consolatory 'topics' were employed – and employed deliberately – by some of the other
major poets of the century.

For examples of consolatory 'topics' addressed specifically to
the bereaved we need look no further than Chaucer. The most
conspicuous examples occur in *The Knight's Tale*, where both
Egeus and Theseus offer words of consolation after the death of
Arcite. It is true that these speeches are based upon passages in
Boccaccio or Boethius. But Professor Cross has noticed that
Chaucer introduces into Theseus's speech a consolatory 'topic'
that occurs in neither of his main sources:

' "The grete tounes se we wane and wende" ' (A.3025)[38]

The reader must be referred to Professor Cross's article for an
explanation of how this sentiment became one of the standard
'topics' of consolation. The point to be emphasized here is that
Chaucer's independent introduction of the 'topic' into this
context implies that he was well aware of the peculiar *genre* to

which Theseus's oration belongs and must have recognized the traditional *solacia* in his main sources for what they are.

At A.2837 ff., just after Arcite has died, Chaucer remarks that nobody could 'gladen' Theseus except for his old father, Egeus, who was familiar with 'this worldes transmutacioun'. The author's comment at the end of Egeus's famous speech indicates the *genre* to which it belongs:

> 'And over al this yet seyde he muchel moore
> To this effect, ful wisely to enhorte
> The peple that they sholde hem reconforte.'[39]
>
> (A.2850–52)

In the course of the seven lines of his speech Egeus is made to utter three traditional *solacia*: Death is the common lot of man (2843–46); life in this world is but a pilgrimage (2847–48); 'Deeth is an ende of every worldly soore' (2849). The last of these occurs in Seneca, *Consolatio ad Marciam*,[40] and is used by St. Basil for the purpose of consolation. Basil also employs the topic that life is only a journey[41] – and so does Seneca.[42] Much of Theseus's address at A.2987 ff. is likewise compounded of consolatory topics, including the one already used by Egeus in A.2849. This is immediately followed, in ll. 3027–34, by an amplified version of 'death is the common lot of man' which includes the familiar rhetorical formula for describing the variety of ways in which a man may meet his death:

> ' "Som in his bed, som in the depe see,
> Som in the large feeld, as men may see . . ." '

The next topic to be elaborated (3035–46) is the futility of striving against the will of God – 'Juppiter' in this pagan context – and the benefits to be derived from patience. As part of this *locus communis* comes the advice to 'maken vertue of necessitee'. Finally, in ll. 3047–56, we find the *solacium* of the *opportunitas mortis* which, like practically all the other consolatory 'topics' in these speeches, occurs in the antique rather than the Christian version: it is more honourable for a man to die when his reputation is at its height than 'whan his name apalled is for age'.

The Tale of Melibee is derived at one remove from the thirteenth-century *Liber Consolationis et Consilii* of Albertanus of

Brescia. In Chaucer's translation of the French paraphrase of
this work there is much more counsel than consolation, and it is
only the opening of the tale that is relevant to the present
argument. Melibee's enemies had attacked his daughter 'and
laften hire for deed'. He pessimistically does not consider the
possibility of her recovering from her wounds and 'lyk a mad
man, rentynge his clothes, gan to wepe and crie'. His wife,
Prudence, after allowing him a certain period of lamentation,
proceeds to console him primarily with the topic of the folly of
immoderate grief. The topic is developed at considerable length
(down to B.2190) and is supported by citations from Old and
New Testaments (including the almost inevitable *Job* i, 21);
from Seneca, whom we have already encountered as one of the
ancient masters of consolation; and – somewhat surprisingly –
from Ovid's *Remedia Amoris*.

It is fitting that the *solacia* uttered by the pagan characters in
The Knight's Tale should be of the antique kind and that in
The Tale of Melibee there should be both pagan and Christian
examples. Since *The Book of the Duchess* was addressed by a
Christian author to a fellow Christian who was mourning the
death of his wife, one might have expected it to be a mine of
consolatory topics of the Christian kind.[43] But none of the
arguments with which the dreamer attempts to comfort the
black knight are religious,[44] and the most cogent of the indirect
consolations that Chaucer addresses to John of Gaunt is merely
to remind him that Fortune was favourable to him in making
him the successful wooer of such a lady as Blanche.[45] Although
Chaucer hints at the possibility of consolation, he has too much
sensitivity and too much respect for the mourner's grief to
suppose that he can succeed in consoling a man who is suffering
the agony of bereavement; and he has sufficient tact not to try.
What he does attempt is to build a monument in honour of the
duchess and to offer sympathy to her husband – which is not
consolation according to the traditions of the *genre*. This
expression of sympathy is subtly achieved by demonstrating the
inadequacy of attempted consolation. At the end of the dream
the would-be consoler is reduced to exclaiming helplessly: 'Is
that youre los? By God, hyt ys routhe.' (l. 1310). Then Chaucer
immediately introduces a device to bring the dream to an end,
so that dreamer and reader alike may escape from the intoler-

able atmosphere of bereavement; but the mourner must remain there solitary and unconsoled.[46]

Because his intention is to render the dreamer's consolation ultimately ineffective, Chaucer refrains from putting into his mouth any of the Christian *solacia* that occur in *Pearl*; but he employs several of the well-worn classical 'topics'. One of these is the 'topic' of the futility of immoderate grief. At ll. 722 ff. he describes – with the aid of classical *exempla* and the solitary Biblical instance of Samson – how such grief may drive a man to suicide and damnation. Like the mourner in *Pearl*, the knight had denounced Fortune as a 'false thef' (l. 650) for stealing from him his lady, who is here represented metaphorically as the 'fers' in a game of chess. The dreamer administers a *solacium* that was a specific for complaints against Fortune: at ll. 715 ff. he bids the knight remember how Socrates took no account of anything that Fortune could do to him. But he stops short at this Stoical argument and does not proceed to the explicitly Christian consolation, which the author of *Pearl* employs; namely, that what appears to us to be the arbitrary dealing of Fortune is really an act of Divine Providence and should be borne in patience. In any case, this commonplace remedy sounds particularly trite and platitudinous, coming as it does after the knight has himself half humorously answered his own complaint by saying that he can hardly blame Fortune for the theft; had he been in her position he would have done the same (ll. 675 ff.).

I have already remarked that Boccaccio's *Olympia* comes nearer to *Pearl* than does *The Book of the Duchess*. Yet Christian consolation is not the driving force in this eclogue as it is in *Pearl*. There is no advance from a mourner's rebellious grief to a state of hopeful resignation. Near the beginning of the poem Camalus refers to Sylvius's lamentation; but the latter seems just as determined to continue his lamentations after the vision of Olympia has been granted him.[47] Nevertheless, it is worth observing that Olympia herself employs several consolatory topics at one point in the dialogue with her earthly father (between ll. 146–54).[48]

My final example is perhaps the most interesting of all. In *Convivio* ii, 13 Dante describes his reaction to the death of Beatrice:

'. . . when I lost the first delight of my soul, whereof mention is made above, I was pierced by so great sorrow that no comfort availed me. Yet after a certain time my mind, which was casting about to heal itself, made proof (since neither my own consolation nor that of others availed) to fall back upon the manner which a certain disconsolate one had erst followed to console himself. And I set myself to read that book of Boethius, not known to many, wherein, a captive and an exile, he had consoled himself. And hearing further that Tully had written another book wherein, treating *Of Friendship*, he had touched upon words of the consolation of Lelius, a man of highest excellence, on the death of Scipio his friend, I set myself to reading it. And although it was at first difficult for me to enter into their meaning, finally I entered as deeply into it as my command of Latin, and what little wit I had, enabled me to do; by which wit I already began to perceive many things as in a dream; as may be seen in the *Vita Nuova*.'[49]

Dante's reference to Cicero is interesting because he occupies a particularly important place in the history of the *genre* in antiquity.[50]

Dante introduces this passage into the *Convivio* to explain how his interest in philosophy began. But, as every reader of his works knows, Dante's ultimate consolation for the death of Beatrice did not come from Philosophy, the 'donna gentile', or from pagan specialists in consolation; but from Beatrice herself and Christian revelation.[51] It consisted partly in the knowledge that Beatrice was in Heaven, but also of something beyond that. In the *Paradiso* Beatrice acts as Dante's guide to an end that lies beyond herself; even as guide she is eventually replaced by St. Bernard, who prepares Dante for the Beatific Vision. The function of Beatrice in this scheme may remind the reader of the 'topic', common in Christian consolations, that the deceased, having been received into Heaven, may intercede for the salvation of the bereaved. It is also similar to the pattern of consolation to be found in *Pearl*.

Consolation was only one of many motives that played their part in the genesis of the *Commedia*; whereas in *Pearl* it is the primary purpose. On the available evidence it is impossible to be absolutely certain whether or not the English poet was aware

C

of the *consolatio* as a distinctive *genre*, although both internal and external evidence suggest that he very probably was. There can, however, be no doubt that it makes better sense of the poem to describe it as a consolation than an elegy. When comparing *Pearl* with some of the fourth-century examples of the *genre*, Mr Watts observes that they too contain a considerable amount of doctrinal and theological material.[52] But he also observes – as, indeed, does Favez – that in these early Christian consolations the doctrinal material is often to be found in digressions whose relevance to the work's primary purpose is far from apparent. I shall argue that all the doctrinal material in *Pearl* is directed towards its main purpose of consolation.

CHAPTER TWO

Structure

It is generally recognized that *Pearl* is the most highly wrought
and intricately constructed poem in Middle English. My main
purpose in this chapter is to examine the relationship between
its structure and its meaning. It will be convenient to distinguish between what may be called its external and its
interior structure. The former consists of the pattern made by
the grouping and linking of stanzas; the latter of the *dispositio* of
the poem's argument, which forms an even more significant
pattern.

(i) THE EXTERNAL STRUCTURE

M. Edgar de Bruyne has shown how important as a basis for
patristic and medieval theories of aesthetic was the text from
Wisdom xi, 21: 'Omnia in mensura et numero et pondere
disposuisti.'[1] *Pearl*, with its ordered and well balanced con-
struction, based to some extent upon numerical factors, illustrates part of this ideal more clearly than any other Middle
English poem. The best known example of a medieval poem
that exhibits this same ideal is, of course, Dante's *Commedia*,
where the number Three not only provides the organizing
principle for the rhyme-scheme, the number of cantos and of
cantiche, but also has a symbolic significance. C. O. Chapman's
attempt to discover a similar trinitarian key to the structure of
Pearl, though interesting in some of its details, is unconvincing
as a whole.[2] But, since Chapman's article appeared, E. R.
Curtius has reminded us that numerical composition in the
Middle Ages made use of other numbers besides Three; in
particular he has shown that authors had a predilection for
'round' numbers – that is, any number divisible by Five.[3] Such
'round' numbers have an obvious aesthetic appeal and this may
be a sufficient reason for the scheme of 20 groups of 5 stanzas in

Pearl. Readers of Sir Thomas Browne may suspect that there is also some 'mystical' reason for the poet's choice. It may be relevant that in l. 451, and again in l. 849, Five is used in a colloquial expression as a multiplier that will produce an infinitely large number (of heavenly rewards). In *Sir Gawain and the Green Knight* we are told that the pentacle is known in English as the 'endeles knot'; as the device on the hero's shield it symbolizes *trawþe*, a comprehensive virtue which includes integrity, flawlessness and perfection.[4] All these qualities are obviously relevant to the meaning of *Pearl*.

Professor Norman Davis has drawn our attention to another numerical association between these two texts in the same MS.: in both poems the total number of stanzas is 101.[5] Whether the number had any intrinsic significance I do not know, but the coincidence suggests that the presence in Group XV of six stanzas, instead of the regular five, may be intentional and that editors have been misguided in their attempts to decide which one should be cancelled. A recent article by Miss P. M. Kean gives substantial support to this view.[6] Assuming that none of the stanzas in this group is superfluous, Miss Kean asks why the poet should introduce the number 6 into a system of grouping that is based upon the number 5. Her answer is, in brief, that it is meant to draw attention to the importance in the poem of its multiple, 12. There are twelve lines in each stanza and the total number of lines in the poem is 1212. Twelve is a number of great importance in the Apocalyptic account of the dimensions (and other features) of the New Jerusalem, all of which are recorded by our poet. Likewise the number 1212 becomes significant – Miss Kean argues – if one considers it as 'twelve *and* twelve'. Presumably she also means 'twelve *times* twelve', because the square of this number, 144, gives us (in thousands) the number of 'vergyneȝ' who follow the Lamb in the procession through the New Jerusalem. The remainder of Miss Kean's article is concerned to show why the author should choose Group XV as the one to be given six stanzas. Although I find some of her arguments on this point unconvincing, one piece of evidence that she adduces is interesting: Group XV contains stanza 72, and 72 is a multiple of 12. This fact, however, becomes far more interesting if it is considered in relation to another which Miss Kean appears to have overlooked. As a result of the additional stanza the total number of lines in Group XV is also 72. Moreover, this particular multiple of twelve happens to be half of 144.[7] Thus the number of stanzas in Group XV is half the 'Apocalyptic' number, 12, and the total number of lines in the group is half 144 – the only other 'Apocalyptic' number that has any important place in the poem.

The numerical structure of *Pearl* consists, therefore, of a marriage of two systems: one is based upon Five, the other upon Twelve – both of them numbers that carry a symbolic significance relevant to the content of the poem.[8] So far this investigation of the poet's use of the mystical mathematics of the city of Heaven has been concerned with his use of celestial arithmetic; I now venture to make some speculations about his employment of celestial 'geometry' – if the oxymoron be permitted. Miss Everett has remarked that the effect of a completed circle that is given by the poet's use of concatenation is 'intended perhaps to suggest the idea of the pearl, which in l. 738 is called "endeleȝ rounde" '.[9] This may indeed have been the poet's intention. But it should be recalled that when he describes the pearl as 'endeleȝ rounde' his particular reason for doing so is to explain why it is 'lyke þe reme of heuenesse clere' (l. 735). The circular form of the poem may therefore also be intended to represent the sphere of the heavenly kingdom. A passage towards the end of the *Roman de la Rose* may be cited in support of this suggestion. In this passage the true heavenly paradise is contrasted with the garden of Deduit (the park of *amour courtois*) which Guillaume de Lorris, in the earlier portion of the poem, had described as paradise. This false paradise, Deduit's garden, is there described as square; but the true paradise:

' "Ainz est si ronde e si soutille
Qu'onques ne fu beriz ne bille
De fourme si bien arondie." '   (ll. 20295–97)[10]

There is, however, an alternative explanation: the poem's circular form may be intended to represent the perfect sphere of Heaven without any intermediary reference to the solitary pearl of great price. My reason for suspecting this is that, if the external form of *Pearl* is indeed intended to be a kind of τεχνο-παίγνιον[11] (though in a less obviously graphic way than George Herbert's 'The Altar' or 'Easter Wings'), the visual image that it suggests is not so much that of a single, solid and spherical pearl as of something that consists of a number of linked units – such as a necklace of pearls. It is perhaps not too fanciful to regard each stanza as the equivalent of a single pearl in a necklace. But there is a complicating factor. In the poem the stanzas are grouped in fives, with the result that a more exact counterpart in the realm of jewellery would be a rosary, in which the beads are similarly distributed in groups. Rosaries of pearls are not unknown and it is no improbable conjecture that they would have been popular in the fourteenth century, which has been described as the pearl age *par excellence*.[12] Admittedly, the beads of a rosary are grouped in decades, not in pentads, and the number of decades, although it was not always five or fifteen as is usual today, is unlikely to have been as large as the number of stanza-groups in *Pearl*.[13] Nor have the various devotional 'mysteries' of the Rosary much relevance to the subject-matter of our poem. But it is not my contention that *Pearl* is meant to exhibit the form of the Rosary; I wish to suggest only that it has the form of some object consisting of pearls that are grouped in a similar way to the beads in a rosary.

The question that has now to be answered is whether there is any evidence for supposing that such an artifact, in which gems or pearls were disposed in this way, could have been regarded as a symbol of 'þe reme of heuenesse clere'. A possible answer may be found in the iconographical symbolism of a kind of ecclesiastical chandelier, known as a *corona*, whose relevance to the argument of *Pearl* I have discussed elsewhere.[14] These candelabra consisted basically of a gilded circle set with gems or pearls: the circle represented the New Jerusalem, and the *cordons* of pearls ranged round its outer circumference symbolized the virtuous souls who inhabit the heavenly city. In one such candelabrum the basic circle is divided into eight lobes and in all the larger examples the circle is broken at regular intervals by the 'towers' carrying the oil-lamps. The effect of this on the *cordons* of pearls was perhaps to produce a pattern similar to that to be found in the rosary, where the 'Ave' beads are grouped into decades as the result of the regular interruption by the 'gaudies'. This effect is also not unlike that which is imposed upon the stanza-linking in *Pearl* by the additional complication of stanza-grouping. An important strand in the 'plot' of the poem virtually comes to an end at l. 1186 where the dreamer rejoices in the knowledge that his pearl has after all been set in such a *garlande* or *corona*; which is an allegorical representation of the fact that the child's soul is safe in the New Jerusalem. What I would now suggest is that the external form of the poem may celebrate this fact which the dreamer has learnt from his vision. The poet has constructed a kind of *corona* by his use of *concatenatio*, in which each stanza perhaps represents a pearl. Such a figure would certainly provide an appropriate setting for his own beloved and beatified pearl.

There is one other fact that may be relevant to this argument.[15] The term *corona* (or *crown* or *garland*) was used by sixteenth-century English and Italian poets to designate a kind of sonnet sequence linked by *concatenatio*. *OED* cites an example from Sidney's *Arcadia* (1580) 217, under *Crown* sb. †32: 'A kind of verse, in which the last line of each stanza is repeated to head the next stanza'. There are other secular examples, but the form and the title were also used for religious verse – the most familiar example being Donne's *La Corona*. Professor Louis L. Martz[16] associates the devotional poems written in this form with the kind of rosary known as the 'Corona of our Lady'. Donne's poem consists of seven ten-line stanzas corresponding to the seven decades of this type of rosary. Not only are the stanzas linked by concatenation, but (as in *Pearl*) the end of the sequence is linked to the beginning by the same method. Unfortunately, I have not come across any instances where the word *corona* is used to describe such a verse form as early as the fourteenth century. It must also be admitted that, according to the *Catholic Encyclopaedia*, the 'Crown of Our Lady' or 'Franciscan' rosary (with seven decades, instead of the five or fifteen of the 'Dominican' rosary) goes back only to 1422.

Whether this hypothesis proves to be tenable, or whether the simpler suggestion – supported by the passage from the *Roman de la Rose* – is preferred, there seems little doubt that the external form of *Pearl* is meant to be a kind of τεχνο-παίγνιον or 'game of art' and that it is based to some extent upon principles of numerical composition.

(ii) THE INTERIOR STRUCTURE

My analysis of the poem's external structure may have tempted the reader to suspect that Virtuosity was the one pearl of great price, to obtain which the poet was content to sacrifice everything else. But this external form is an added grace that does not interfere with the essential development of the argument.[17] A comparable ingenuity and neatness of design are evident in what I call the 'interior structure'; that is, the arrangement of the argument itself. Here again, however, it is true to say that the progress and the meaning of the argument are in no way distorted by the partial symmetry of its *dispositio*.

Miss Everett has observed the way in which, as in *Sir Gawain and the Green Knight*,

> '. . . the matter of *Pearl* is ordered so as to form a pattern. Naturally the means by which this is done here differ from those employed in the narrative poem, and the pattern is all-embracing, as it is not in *Sir Gawain*. Of the twenty equal sections of the poem the first four are mainly devoted to presenting the dreamer's state of mind and to description of the dream-country and of Pearl herself; argument and exposition occupy the central twelve sections, and the last four again contain description, this time of the New Jerusalem, and end with the poet's reflections. This pattern is emphasized by the echoing of the first line of the poem, "Perle plesaunte to prynces paye" in the last, "Ande precious perleȝ vnto his pay".'[18]

Readers who are interested in numerological composition will not fail to notice the way in which the importance of Twelve and its factor Four is brought out in this admirably concise summary. Nevertheless, it is perhaps better to think of the first and last stanza-groups, which describe the mourner's waking experience, separately from those in which the dream is recounted. Whereas there is correspondence between the two descriptions, there is a marked contrast between the attitudes of the mourner before and after his vision: in the first stanza-group he is grief-stricken, rebellious and despondent; in the final group his mood is one of chastened resignation, self-criticism and hope. The three sections devoted to description, with which the account of the vision begins, correspond to the three with which it ends to an even greater extent than Miss Everett suggests. For, not only does the description of the dream-country culminate in the appearance of the maiden and the dreamer's partial recognition of her, but that of the New Jerusalem also reaches its climax when the dreamer recognizes his 'lyttel quene' among the other 'maydeneȝ' in the heavenly procession.

There is yet another refinement in the patterning of the interior structure that Miss Everett's summary does not mention: the debate that occupies the twelve central sections is itself divided into two parts that correspond as far as their subject-matter is concerned, though they are not of equal length. The first part of this debate is mostly concerned with the maiden's claim to be a queen in heaven; the second with her assertion that she is a bride of the Lamb. At ll. 769 ff. we hear the dreamer's reactions to her statement that she is a bride of the Lamb:

> ' "Why, maskelleȝ bryd þat bryȝt con flambe,
> Þat reieteȝ hatȝ so ryche and ryf,
> Quat kyn þyng may be þat Lambe
> Þat þe wolde wedde vnto hys vyf?
> Ouer alle oþer so hyȝ þou clambe
> To lede wyth hym so ladyly lyf.
> So mony a comly on-vnder cambe
> For Kryst han lyued in much stryf:
> And þou con alle þo dere out dryf
> And fro þat maryag al oþer depres,
> Al only þyself so stout and styf,
> A makeleȝ may and maskelleȝ." '

These lines correspond to the similar charge of usurpation that he had brought against her on hearing her announcement that she is a queen in Heaven:

> ' "Blysful", quod I, "may þys be trwe?
> Dyspleseȝ not if I speke errour.
> Art þou þe quene of heueneȝ blwe,
> Þat al þys worlde schal do honour?
> We leuen on Marye þat grace of grewe,
> Þat bar a barne of vyrgyn flour;
> Þe croune fro hyr quo moȝt remwe
> Bot ho hir passed in sum fauour?
> Now, for synglerty o hyr dousour,
> We calle hyr Fenyx of Araby,
> Þat freles fleȝe of hyr fasor,
> Lyk to þe Quen of cortaysye." '   (ll. 421–32)

But the second division of the debate is far more condensed than the first, so the stanza beginning at l. 769 also incorporates objections by the dreamer that correspond to those he had advanced in the stanzas beginning at l. 481 and l. 589. Similarly, there are correspondences between the maiden's replies in the two parts of the debate: compare, for example, ll. 445 ff. with ll. 845 ff. and observe especially the verbal echo of l. 451 ('And wolde her coroune3 wern worþe þo fyue') in l. 849 ('Bot vchon enlé we wolde were fyf'). The one part of the debate is, in fact, exactly twice the length of the other: the first part occupies eight groups, the second consists of four. The greater length of the first part is due mainly to its inclusion of the parable of the labourers in the vineyard, which the maiden introduces as an *exemplum* to give Scriptural authority to her argument about the status that she enjoys in Heaven.

The most interesting feature of the poem's interior structure does not become apparent until we consider what happens at the point where the first part of the debate ends and the second begins. For, in the more or less symmetrical *dispositio* that we have been analysing, this is a key point in the design: although it is not the poem's mathematical centre, it is its structural centre. So, if the structure bears any relationship to the meaning, we might expect the poet to have placed something of supreme significance here.

In order to discover whether he does so, it is first necessary to divine where the watershed between the two parts of the debate comes. This point cannot be plotted with mathematical precision because there is a kind of transitional passage into which the first part merges and which also supplies the cue for the second to begin. Although the limits of this transitional passage cannot be fixed with absolute certainty, I would suggest that it begins in the stanza that opens with l. 697, and continues to l. 744: in other words it comprises the last two stanzas of Group XII and the first two of XIII. The way in which the transition is effected will be examined in the next chapter along with other features of the conduct of the debate. What I would draw attention to now is the fact that in ll. 729 ff. occurs the only explicit reference in the poem to the parable of the pearl of great price, and that this is immediately preceded by, and linked to, the sole reference to another passage from the Gospel;

namely, that in which Jesus declares that nobody may enter the Kingdom of Heaven 'Bot he com þyder ryȝt as a chylde' (l. 723).

The allusion to the parable of the pearl of great price is obviously the more important of the two as far as the poem's structure is concerned. Its function in the poem is as radical as that of the *thema* or Biblical text in a learned fourteenth-century sermon constructed according to the principles recommended in the *Artes Praedicandi*. According to the authors of these treatises, the *thema*, enunciated at the beginning of the discourse, was the single root out of which the whole composition was to grow like a tree, branching out into digressions, distinctions and correspondences.[19] But the author of *Pearl*, instead of enunciating his text explicitly at the beginning of his composition, places it at the centre – which is the most important position in a poem whose external structure is nearly circular and whose interior structure is more or less symmetrical. From this central position – the true heart of the poem – the imagery and the *sentence* of the parable permeate the whole structure, reaching out to its periphery or extremities. Only in the light of the parable at the structural centre is it possible to perceive the full meaning of the enigmatic use of the image of the pearl at the beginning of the poem and the true significance of its figurative use at the close.

The implications of the poet's juxtaposing the allusion to the parable and his reference to the episode of Jesus and the children will be examined later. But enough has probably been said already to give some indication of why I maintain that in *Pearl* the structure is part of the meaning.

It may be felt that such a structure, built on principles of correspondence and approximate symmetry, is more appropriate for the visual arts and too static for a work of literature that must unfold itself gradually.[20] But *Pearl* is not the only fourteenth-century English poem in which argument and narrative are subjected to more or less symmetrical patterning. In *Piers Plowman* there are correspondences between the ploughing episodes in B.vi and xix and between B. Prologue and the final Passus xx. Even in the lengthy narrative of *Troilus and Criseyde* there are carefully contrived correspondences between earlier and later episodes and, as Miss Everett has shown,[21] a careful 'patterning' of material is to be found in *Sir Gawain and the Green Knight* which, far from impeding the narrative, makes it more pointed and significant. Similarly in *Pearl*, the scrupulously patterned *dispositio* is never allowed to interfere with the progress and development of the argument. The pointed contrast between the dreamer's attitudes in the first and final stanza-groups, which has already been noticed, is a measure of the progress towards spiritual wisdom that he makes in the course of the poem. The continuing development of his character is one of the principal means by which the action advances.[22]

However orderly the *dispositio* of the argument may be, the dreamer's progress is certainly not made in an orderly fashion, but reveals his considerable instability of character. His mood alternates between extremes of despair and elation, humility and presumption, with the occasional interlude of sober attentiveness. Eventually his impetuosity causes him to be 'kaste of kyþeȝ þat lasteȝ aye' and to find himself back in the 'doel-doungoun' of this world. Only after he has sustained this chastening experience does he learn true wisdom and resignation to the Divine Will. These fluctuations in the dreamer's moods and attitudes are thrown into relief by the contrast with the serenity and imperturbability of the maiden's character. The poet is here faced with the problem of how to avoid making the maiden appear a prig and the dreamer seem a fool. He manages this successfully, except that we perhaps become a little impatient of the dreamer's obstinate literal-mindedness by the time we reach ll. 919 ff. and find him unable to believe that Jerusalem can be situated amid the paradisal landscape, since its proper place is 'in Judee'.

Although the carefully patterned structure does not impede the linear progress of the action or the argument, a few unsatisfactory features appear to result from the necessity of introducing a second part of the debate that corresponds in some ways to the first, and more especially from the need to introduce a second description that occupies, like the first one, three whole stanza-groups. Many readers have probably felt that the quality of the poet's inspiration deteriorates in the second part of the account of the vision. They would, no doubt, admit that he was wise to make the latter part of the debate only half the length of the first; especially as it is sustained for most of its course by means of the common exegetical device of an allegorical *distinctio* concerning the significance of Jerusalem and of the Lamb. But it is the description of the New Jerusalem that the modern reader probably finds the least satisfactory part of the poem. The enumeration of the foundation stones of the city causes the author to lapse into a passage of barren *amplificatio* by means of a catalogue – a device that medieval poets often resorted to, but one that is unworthy of this poet. Yet that is only a temporary lapse: the main criticism is that, in spite of some felicitous modifications of the poet's principal source, the whole description amounts to little more than a Biblical paraphrase.

It is of little service to the author to submit the extenuating plea that fear of heterodoxy obliged him to adhere to his sacred source and that he cannot therefore be blamed for inheriting some of the intractable material that abounds in what is, for the modern reader, the least attractive book of the Bible. Any medieval poet's attempt to present a vision of heavenly mysteries inevitably invites comparison with the final cantos of the *Paradiso*, where Dante shows how adherence to ecclesiastical dogma need not preclude originality of presentation or even a complete imaginative re-creation of traditional material. The reader who knows his Dante is therefore likely to find this part of *Pearl* disappointing – at least, at a first reading of it. The poet's recognition of his 'lyttel quene' in the midst of the procession that follows the slightly chimerical figure of the Lamb 'wyth hornez seuen of red golde cler' will remind him not so much of the *Paradiso* as of *Purgatorio* xxx, where Dante sees Beatrice in the midst of the procession that is made up of some rather lifeless, heraldic figures including the awesomely chimerical gryphon.[23] The description of this procession is not generally regarded as one of Dante's more inspired inventions.

A closer examination of the poem, however, will show that some of these criticisms are less justified than they appear to be. The second part of the debate makes a more positive contribution to the argument than might at first be supposed. In their earliest exchanges (in Groups V–VII) the maiden had the negative task of trying to make the dreamer accept the fact that the close ties of kinship that had formerly existed between them are irrevocably broken. The remainder of the first part of the debate consisted of a more abstract argument about Divine Justice and heavenly rewards. In the second part the maiden proceeds to the positive task of revealing that she now enjoys with the Lamb, her *lemman*, an even more intimate relationship than any which she could possibly experience with the dreamer, her earthly father. In this part theological argument is kept to a minimum with the result that the tone is generally more personal and more lyrical. This can perhaps be most easily appreciated if a comparison is made between two passages that are concerned with the Crucifixion; one in the first part and the other in the second. At ll. 645 ff. the maiden describes the remedy for Original Sin:

> ' "Bot þeron com a bote astyt.
> Ryche blod ran on rode so roghe,
> And wynne water þen at þat plyt:
> Þe grace of God wex gret innoghe.
>
> ' "Innoghe þer wax out of þat welle,
> Blod and water of brode wounde.
> Þe blod vus boȝt fro bale of helle
> And delyuered vus of þe deth secounde;
> Þe water is baptem, þe soþe to telle,
> Þat folȝed þe glayue so grymly grounde . . ." '

The narrative is entirely impersonal; the Person Whose blood is shed is not mentioned. Similarly the passing allusion to the Passion at ll. 705–6, although no longer impersonal, remains anonymous:

> ' "Bot he on rode þat blody dyed,
> Delfully þurȝ hondeȝ þryȝt . . ." '

But the stanza beginning at l. 805 is as moving and as intimate as any of the best Middle English lyrics on the Passion (the 'lemman' has been intimately identified in the preceding stanza):

> ' "In Jerusalem watȝ my lemman slayn
> And rent on rode wyth boyeȝ bolde.
> Al oure baleȝ to bere ful bayn,
> He toke on hymself oure careȝ colde.
> Wyth boffeteȝ watȝ hys face flayn
> Þat watȝ so fayr on to byholde.

For synne he set hymself in vayn,
Þat neuer hade non hymself to wolde.
For vus he lette hym flyȝe and folde
And brede vpon a bostwys bem;
As meke as lomp þat no playnt tolde
For vus he swalt in Jerusalem." '

And yet this stanza forms part of the allegorical *distinctio* that
has already been mentioned; the poet's use of this common
exegetical device is not as arid and academic an exercise as one
might suppose.

The *distinctiones* in the second part of the debate prepare us
for the vision of the New Jerusalem. In his description of the
Heavenly City the author is not trying to emulate canto xxxiii of
the *Paradiso*; it is not his intention to deploy all his poetic
powers to enable the reader to experience what it is like to perceive the Beatific Vision. His particular reason for adhering to
the text of the *Apocalypse* is that he wishes to concentrate upon
the aspect of Deity that is most relevant to this poem about a
pure and innocent child who suffered an untimely death. The
climax is not reached with the vision of 'þe hyȝe trone' on which
sits 'þe hyȝe Godeȝ self'; the poet is content to mention this in
passing at a fairly early stage in the description (ll. 1051–54).
The climax does not begin until the appearance of the white
Lamb, the pure, innocent and humble Victim Who voluntarily
suffered an untimely death in order to redeem mankind. He has
saved the maiden, his *lemman*, who, like the other *vergyneȝ* in the
procession, is dressed in His *liuré*: 'As praysed perleȝ hys wedeȝ
wasse' (l. 1112). The dreamer can now see for himself in Whose
likeness she has been re-created and to Whom she rightfully
belongs. When he encountered her at the end of the first
description she was alone and prepared to address him; but,
when he again catches sight of her at the end of the second
description she is happy 'among her fereȝ' – entirely absorbed
in the 'meyny schene' of the Lamb. Having assured the
mourner of her own salvation, and having indicated to him at
the centre of the poem the nature of the only pearl he can hope
to acquire, Pearl has fulfilled her consolatory mission and, in
our last glimpse of her, she appears to be no longer aware of his
presence.

CHAPTER THREE

The Conduct of the Debate

At l. 390, during one of his interludes of genuine humility, the dreamer beseeches the maiden 'wythouten debate' to tell him about the life she leads in her new country. His failure to observe this self-imposed condition is one of the ironies of his characterization. If he had kept his promise, it might well have happened that 'To mo of [Godes] mysterys [he] hade ben dryuen'; but the reader would have been obliged to content himself with an edifying homily from the maiden instead of being entertained by a lively dispute.

The maiden has at her command all the techniques of learned disputation, but uses them without fuss or pretentious- ness: she makes careful distinctions and 'confirms' her arguments by drawing on a wealth of authoritative Scriptural texts. The rapidity with which her analytical mind works is seen in one of her earliest contributions to the dialogue. When the dreamer recognizes his lost pearl, he is overjoyed and im- petuously looks forward to dwelling with her in the delectable country on the further shore of the stream. During his emo- tional outburst, the maiden has silently marked his erroneous statements and added them up. Her reply takes us by surprise:

> ' "Þre wordeȝ hatȝ þou spoken at ene:
> Vnavysed, for soþe, wern alle þre." '   (ll. 291–92)

She then enumerates them one after another. From some of her earlier speeches we may feel that she is a somewhat unsympa- thetic figure who reasons like a 'school divine'; but we soon discover that she is more akin to Dante's Beatrice than to Milton's God.

The apparently inexhaustible supply of texts in her armoury ranges from the extended narrative of the labourers in the vine- yard – which she cites as an *exemplum* – to the citation of a single verse from a Psalm or some other book of the Bible. These brief quotations often have the clinching effect of a *sentence* or proverb. Sometimes they are so well integrated into the argument that it is difficult to recognize them as quotations or allusions to Scripture at all. An example of this is the *sentence* used as the refrain for Section XI: 'For þe grace of God is gret innoghe', which editors have failed to recognize as an allusion to II *Corinthians* xii, 9: 'My grace is sufficient for thee: for my strength is made perfect in weakness.' But it may also have acquired gnomic status by the fourteenth century; it was certainly a recognized proverb in the sixteenth century.[1]

The dreamer, on the other hand, finds it difficult to 'distinguish' (between the two Jerusalems, between earthly and heavenly conceptions of royalty – and even between 'maskelleȝ' and 'makeleȝ'). Like Pertelote, who relies upon the paltry Dionysius Cato as her only 'auctour',[2] he bolsters his argument with only a single quotation – though it comes from a perfectly respectable source. But he manipulates this valuable 'piece' with some dexterity until, at the end of the stanza, he believes that he has manoeuvred the maiden into an untenable position:

> 'Then more I meled and sayde apert:
> "Me þynk þy tale vnresounable.
> Goddeȝ ryȝt is redy and euermore rert,
> Oþer Holy Wryt is bot a fable.
> In Sauter is sayd a verce ouerte
> Þat spekeȝ a poynt determynable:
> 'Þou quyteȝ vchon as hys desserte,
> Þou hyȝe kyng ay pretermynable.'
> Now he þat stod þe long day stable,
> And þou to payment com hym byfore,
> Þenne þe lasse in werke to take more able,
> And euer þe lenger þe lasse, þe more." '   (ll. 589–600)

But the maiden has no difficulty in perceiving what he is plotting:

> ' "Bot now þou moteȝ, me for to mate,
> Þat I my peny haf wrang tan here . . ." '   (ll. 613–14)

He was mistaken, if he thought he had her in 'check'; his terrestrial concepts of 'more' and 'less' are irrelevant to the argument:

D

' "Of more and lasse in Godeȝ ryche",
Þat gentyl sayde, "lys no joparde . . ." '   (ll. 601–2)

At ll. 699–700 she introduces a counter-citation from another
psalm with which she eventually 'takes' his prized piece at
ll. 701–4:

' "Forþy to corte quen þou schal com
Þer alle oure causeȝ schal be tryed,
Alegge þe ryȝt, þou may be innome,
*By þys ilke spech I haue asspyed . . ." '
                    (ll. 701–4 – my italics)[3]

But the checkmate that is threatened in these lines is somewhat
more ominous than the prospect of defeat in a disputation. In
the remainder of this chapter I shall concentrate upon the more
serious purpose of this part of the debate as it approaches the
poem's structural centre.

In her interpretation of the parable of the labourers in the
vineyard the maiden seeks to justify to the dreamer the reward
that she has received in Heaven. As far as l. 616 her argument is
concerned explicitly with her own case, but thereafter it becomes more impersonal, dealing with the salvation of 'innocents'
and adults in general terms. It includes a historical exposition
of the scheme of salvation, beginning at l. 637 with an account
of the consequences of Original Sin. The next stanza narrates
the divine remedy for that sin and refers, in particular, to the
institution of the sacrament of baptism, which washes away our
Original Sin:

' "Now is þer noȝt in þe worlde rounde
Bytwene vus and blysse bot þat [Adam] wythdroȝ,
And þat is restored in sely stounde;
And þe grace of God is gret innogh." '   (ll. 657–60)

Those who die immediately after baptism are, therefore, saved
because they remain in a state of grace.

The maiden next refers to the man 'þat synneȝ þenne new';
that is, the baptized Christian who commits what theologians
call 'actual sin'. He may be restored to the state of grace which
he acquired at baptism ('be þurȝ mercy to grace þrytȝ' –
l. 670), but only if he is contrite (cf. ll. 662 and 669):

' "Bot wyth sorȝ and syt he mot hit craue,
And byde þe payne þerto is bent." '   (ll. 663–64)

These lines probably refer to the sacrament of Penance or Confession, which absolves men from 'actual sin', provided that they perform the satisfaction or 'penance' (in the narrower sense) which the priest enjoins ('þe payne þerto is bent'). Such absolution, however, is no guarantee against the possibility of the penitent's falling out of a state of grace in future – as the maiden had already observed in ll. 617 ff. So an adult can never be *certain* of salvation, whereas the infant who dies soon after baptism can.

At ll. 673 ff. the maiden admits that the Scriptures promise salvation to two categories of men: the innocent and the righteous. But her development of this distinction shows how hazardous will be the plight of the man who relies upon his own righteousness to act as his sole advocate on Doomsday. Even for the righteous man the surest hope is to be saved 'By innocens and not by ryȝte' (l. 708): that is, presumably, by re-acquiring through prayer and through the sacraments the state of grace that had been bestowed on him at baptism.

In the next two stanzas the maiden confirms her arguments by quoting the words of Jesus Himself. The first of these stanzas confirms her argument about the salvation of infants by referring to the episode of Jesus and the children and by quoting His words: 'To suche is heuenryche arayed' (l. 719). The second confirms her argument about the surest way to salvation – even for adults – by quoting His saying that no man can enter His kingdom 'Bot he com þyder ryȝt as a chylde' (l. 723). This explicit statement about the place of children in Heaven, quoted from the Highest Authority, provides an apt and pointed conclusion to the maiden's justification of the reward she has received. We might expect it also to constitute the climax of her speech; but the statement about the way to enter Heaven prompts her to cite another pronouncement on the subject by 'þe Fader of folde and flode'; namely, the parable of the pearl of great price. In this way the long argument about heavenly rewards, in the course of which no reference has been made to the image of the pearl, is attached to the *thema* at the very heart of the poem.

As the maiden's argument approaches the poem's structural and dynamic centre it undergoes a change that has not yet been mentioned. As already noted, up to l. 616 the maiden is primarily concerned with her own case, but from that point the argument becomes more impersonal, a statement of the doctrinal issues in general terms. At l. 701 it becomes personal again, but now it refers to the case of the dreamer:

> ' "Forþy to corte quen þou schal com
> Þer alle oure causeȝ schal be tryed,
> Alegge þe ryȝt, þou may be innome,
> By þys ilke spech I haue asspyed:
> Bot he on rode þat blody dyed,
> Delfully þurȝ hondeȝ þryȝt,
> Gyue þe to passe, when þou arte tryed,
> By innocens and not by ryȝte." ' (ll. 701–8 – my italics)

When we reach the very heart of the poem we find that the maiden is even more particularly concerned with the dreamer's own spiritual welfare and continues to employ the familiar, singular form of the second personal pronoun. She brings her long speech to its conclusion at the end of the stanza that refers to the pearl of great price. Her closing words are:

> ' "I rede þe forsake þe worlde wode
> And porchace þy perle maskelles." '
> (ll. 743–44 – my italics)

So what began as a defence of her heavenly reward against the dreamer's carping criticisms is skilfully turned by the maiden into a warning about his own plight and ends as an exhortation to him to seek his own reward by imitating, as far as possible, the virtues that she exemplifies.

After this climax the intensity gradually diminishes. The dreamer's questions in the stanza beginning at l. 745 show that he has not really grasped the full significance of the maiden's words about the pearl, although he maintains a mood of genuine wonder throughout this stanza. However, by ll. 773 ff. we find him once again cavilling at the maiden's account of her status in heaven – this time because she claims that the Lamb has espoused her. In the preceding chapter some suggestions were made to account for the fact that the second part of the debate is only half the length of the first. But what is perhaps the principal reason was not mentioned there. The maiden's status as bride of the Lamb, which she assumes by virtue of her virginity, is something that her earthly father obviously cannot hope to emulate. On the other hand, it is possible for him to become a king in Heaven, just as the maiden has become a queen in that kingdom, by recovering through Divine Grace the status that was bestowed upon him at baptism, but which he lost by committing the 'actual sin' that even the righteous man cannot avoid.[4] It is not surprising that the major part of the debate should concentrate on that aspect of the maiden's character which is relevant to the dreamer's own salvation. It is equally fitting that this Christian *consolatio* should contrive to introduce at the climax of the debate, and at the heart of the poem, not only an assurance that the child is beatified, but also an indication to the mourner of the only way in which he can acquire the ultimate consolation that is offered to Christians.

PART TWO

ALLEGORY AND SYMBOLISM

Introductory

'But seek ye first the image of the pearl, and its allegorical significance; and the meaning of all things else in the poem shall be added unto you.' These words, adapted from *Matthew* vi, 33, would appear to be the motto of several writers who have offered interpretations of *Pearl*. It is not surprising that, by following a precept derived from such a source, they have produced interpretations of the most edifying kind; but it is hardly less surprising that readings of the poem which follow such an obsessive principle have proved to be myopic and over-simplified. Having fixed upon a particular meaning for the pearl, each of these interpreters is content to be bounded in his chosen oyster-shell and yet count himself sovereign over the meaning of the whole poem.

The procedure that I adopt in my analysis of the poet's use of allegory and symbolism is almost the opposite of that which I have just described. I believe that any attempt to grasp the meaning of the pearl is bound to be frustrated unless one has first unravelled the various strands of allegory and symbolism that are woven into the poem's intricate texture. Indeed, I maintain that, as soon as these complexities are sorted out, the function and meaning of the image of the pearl become almost self-evident.

For the purpose of my analysis I have tried, as far as possible, to adopt terminology that was current in the thirteenth and fourteenth centuries – although it has been necessary to supplement this with some designations of my own in order to make distinctions that were not explicitly recognized in the theoretical writings of that time. Of the distinctions that were insisted upon by later medieval theorists, the most important was undoubtedly the one which they drew between the two kinds of allegory that are generally known to medievalists as the 'allegory of the theologians' and the 'allegory of the poets'. These terms are adapted from Dante's celebrated remarks in *Convivio* II, i.

I use the term 'allegory of the poets' in a broader sense than Dante does in that passage: what I understand by it is any allegorical or symbolical device that does not fall within the definition of the 'allegory of the theologians'. The theologians themselves used the word 'allegory' in both a broad and a narrow sense: they employed it to refer not only to the *sensus spiritualis* of Scripture, but also to indicate one of the three divisions of that 'sense' – the one known specifically as the *sensus allegoricus*. One other preliminary observation is worth making: neither the 'theologians' on the one hand, nor the 'poets' and rhetoricians on the other, appear to have had much use for any formal distinction between 'allegory' and 'symbolism'; whereas such a distinction provides the starting point for many modern discussions of allegory[1] – including medieval allegory.

CHAPTER FOUR

The 'Allegory of the Theologians'

(i) THE 'ALLEGORY OF THE THEOLOGIANS' AND THE 'ALLEGORY OF THE POETS'

By the designation 'allegory of the theologians' is meant the method that was used by some patristic and many medieval commentators to discover the 'spiritual' sense of Scripture. Today its best remembered feature is its interpretation of the Biblical text according to four 'senses': these were usually defined as the 'literal', the 'allegorical', the 'tropological' or 'moral' and the 'anagogical' or 'mystical'. But this 'polysemous' method of interpretation was not, in fact, peculiar to the Biblical commentators and theologians: it was also employed by poets in commentaries on their own works or on those of other secular authors. Dante in the second treatise of the *Convivio* proposes to offer such a fourfold exposition of his own *canzone*: 'Voi che intendendo il terzo ciel movete'; and he emphasizes the fact that he is following the method of the poets and not that of the theologians – at least as far as the 'senso allegorico' is concerned (*Conv.* II, i). It is true that, in practice, he provides expositions of the *canzone* according to two 'senses' only: he explains, for example, that 'the third heaven' refers literally to the sphere of the planet Venus but that, according to the 'allegorical and true' meaning, it signifies Rhetoric. Nevertheless, in the first chapter of the treatise he had shown how the fourfold method was to be applied to literature generally. In the Epistle to Can Grande della Scala (which, however, may not be authentic) he asserts that the fourfold method should be employed in the interpretation of his *Commedia* – although again hardly any practical indication is given of how it should be applied to the text of the poem. In the *De Genealogia Gentilium Deorum* Boccaccio often adopts the fourfold method in his exposition of classical myths.[1]

If the use of the 'four senses' is not the distinctive feature of the 'method of the theologians', what is? Most medieval theologians would probably have answered this question by pointing to the distinction between allegories *in verbis* and allegories *in facto* – about which more will be said presently. But it must be admitted that many attempts were made to formulate a satisfactory definition of the 'spiritual' sense of the Bible and that there is considerable variation between one definition and another, so that it is impossible to select one that could be claimed as representative. Nevertheless, as might be expected, one of the most penetrating and lucid formulations was made by Aquinas; it is also particularly relevant for our purpose because it distinguishes this kind of allegory from that of the poets. Near the beginning of his *Summa Theologiae*, St. Thomas asks whether it is fitting that Holy Scripture should make use of metaphors, since metaphors are employed by poets, who are concerned with fiction rather than fact and have been denounced as liars. How can the Bible reveal the Truth if it harbours such devices?

Before we consider Aquinas's answer it should be observed that whatever he says about metaphor will apply – with a few modifications that do not affect the present stage of our argument – to poetic allegory and symbolism generally; allegory, as we shall see in the next chapter,[2] was regularly defined as 'translatio continuata' – 'extended, or continued metaphor'.

Aquinas answers the objection by remarking that Holy Scripture has two kinds of author: a Divine Author and various human authors who are inspired by Him. In order to make the Truth known to other men, these human authors of the books of the Bible use metaphorical and figurative language just as poets and other secular writers do. There is, however, one difference between the practice of the authors of the Bible and that of other human authors: whereas a poet uses metaphors 'propter repraesentationem' which is naturally delightful to man, the Biblical author employs them 'propter necessitatem et utilitatem'.[3]

The supreme vindication of the use of metaphorical expression is the fact that it was employed by Jesus Himself in His parables. Nowadays when we consider parables and fables we usually speak of their superficial narrative as the 'literal' sense and their 'hidden meaning' as the allegorical sense. This was also the usual practice in patristic and medieval commentaries: it can be seen, for example, in discussions of parables from Augustine to the thirteenth-century scholastic philosopher, Ulrich of Strasbourg.[4] It can also be seen in Dante's interpretation – in *Conv.* II, i – of Ovid's version of the story of Orpheus taming the wild beasts with the music of his lyre. The literal sense of this fable is a 'bella menzogna' that cloaks its 'allegorical or true' meaning; namely, that the wise man with the instrument of his voice makes cruel hearts gentle and humble. Aquinas, however, in his discussion of the 'sensus parabolicus'[5] differs from these writers in his use of terminology, so that, at first sight, he may appear to be saying the opposite of what they assert. For St. Thomas, the literal sense is not what the words of the fiction signify immediately, but the truth which that signification, in its turn, adumbrates. In other words, the 'sensus litteralis' is the 'hidden meaning' of the parable and not the cloak of fiction that envelops it. A literal statement may be made either 'properly' (*proprie*) or figuratively; the 'sensus parabolicus', which is identical with the 'allegory of the poets', affords a figurative expression of the literal statement.[6] He then gives an example which shows that this 'sensus parabolicus' is not concerned simply with what are nowadays called parables, but includes the use of metaphorical language elsewhere in the Bible:

> 'Non enim cum Scriptura nominat Dei brachium, est litteralis sensus quod in Deo sit membrum huiusmodi corporale, sed id quod per hoc membrum significatur, scilicet virtus operativa. In quo patet quod sensui litterali Sacrae Scripturae numquam potest subesse falsum.'[7]

In this Biblical example a supernatural quality (God's operative power) is presented figuratively by a corporeal image (His arm); but it is also possible to present figuratively a terrestrial, historical event. So, in the opening stanzas of *Pearl*, the 'historical' event of the child's death and burial is presented figuratively in the guise of a fabulous narrative of a pearl that disappeared into the grass.

Whatever objections there may be to Aquinas's different use of terminology, it has one great advantage: it makes much clearer the essential difference between the 'allegory of the poets' and that of the theologians than earlier definitions do. In the definitions by other theologians the term 'sensus litteralis' is used inconsistently: it refers to one thing when they speak of the 'allegory of the poets' but to something else when they speak of the *sensus spiritualis* of the Bible. St. Thomas's usage is entirely consistent. According to his account, the 'sensus litteralis' or 'sensus historicus' is, in effect, what the human authors of Scripture produce. It narrates historical events or makes statements of fact. These narratives and statements may be made either 'properly' (*proprie*) or figuratively. If they are made figuratively the 'sensus parabolicus' or 'allegory of the poets' is involved. But, as we have already seen, in either case the expression is part of the literal sense. The Bible, on the other hand, differs from all other books in that it also has a Divine Author Who is able to express Himself not only through words, as human authors do, but through the very historical events and facts to which the literal sense refers.[8] So the historical facts narrated in the Bible can themselves be allegories of other facts. Allegories of this kind constitute the *sensus spiritualis* of the theologians. The 'allegory of the poets' or 'sensus parabolicus' involves merely a figure of expression or a 'figure of thought'. But the theologians claimed that the *sensus spiritualis* of the Bible is a 'figure of fact'.

Only when this has been recognized is it possible to understand what is distinctive about the theologians' use of the fourfold method of interpretation. This method was essentially a way of reading the Bible that demonstrated how at the centre of the pattern of Divine revelation lay the accomplishment of the Atonement through the historical fact of the Incarnation. Such a doctrine is implicit in St. Thomas's discussion of the *sensus spiritualis*. After showing how this 'sense' is founded upon the literal, he remarks that it has a threefold division:

> 'For as the Apostle says (*Heb.* x, i) the Old Law is a figure of the New Law, and Dionysius says (*Cael. Hier.* i) *the New Law itself is a figure of future glory*. Again, in the New Law, whatever our Head has done is a type of what we ought to do. Therefore, so far as the things of the Old Law signify the things of the New Law, there is the allegorical sense; so far as the things done in Christ, or so far as the things

which signify Christ, are types of what we ought to do, there is the moral sense. But so far as they signify what relates to eternal glory, there is the anagogical sense.'[9]

So the *sensus allegoricus* is a transitional sense, linking the terrestrial to the heavenly by reference to the historical facts of the Incarnation and Atonement.

We have already seen how the theologians' allegory differs from that of the poets and rhetoricians. But the way in which it is focussed upon this historical event also distinguishes it from another symbolic system that claims to go beyond figures of expression and to be concerned with the revelation of metaphysical truth; namely, the system of the Platonists that regards the phenomena of this world as mere shadows and imperfect copies of the reality of an archetypal world of Ideas.[10] Such a symbolic view of the world comes very close to the *sensus anagogicus* of the theologians; yet we should recall St. Augustine's remark that, in the writings of the Platonists, he read 'In the beginning was the Word', but that he did not find written there, 'And the Word was made flesh and dwelt among us'.[11] The 'allegory of the theologians' is essentially an adaptation of this kind of symbolism to allow for the Christian element of direct revelation through the historical fact of the Incarnation. The distinctions I have made may be summarized in an aphorism: the allegory of the poets and rhetoricians is concerned with the effects of 'words'; the symbolism of the 'Platonists' is focussed upon the concept of the Word; the 'sensus spiritualis' is rooted in the conception of the Word Incarnate.

(ii) AN EXEGETICAL PASSAGE IN *Pearl*

There is one passage in *Pearl* that affords indisputable evidence that the author was familiar with the 'method of the theologians' and that he perfectly understood its essential characteristics. The passage comes between ll. 793 and 960, and is concerned with the associated figures of the Lamb and of Jerusalem. The author does not use the technical terms of the 'sacred science', but it is easy to distinguish the *sensus litteralis* in the Old Testament which passes through the *sensus allegoricus*, fulfilled in the Gospel, in order to reach the *sensus anagogicus* as it is revealed in the *Apocalypse*. The maiden demonstrates how the texts from these three sources 'accord' with one another.

The first of these instances (ll. 793–840), which is concerned with the figure of the Lamb, is not, in the strictest sense, an example of the *sensus spiritualis* for it deals, not with Old Testament events, but with an Old Testament prophecy; however, the method was regularly applied to prophecies. At ll. 797 ff. the maiden cites the words of 'þe profete Ysaye'[12] where he foretells the Passion of Christ, employing the simile of the slaughtered Lamb. This is not a true example of what I have called a 'figure of fact' since it is quite clear from the text that the prophet is not speaking of the slaughter of any 'historical' lamb, which has the further sense of referring 'spiritually' to Christ's death. In the Middle Ages it was believed that the actual *words* were a direct allusion to the future event. The maiden could have introduced an example of an 'allegory of fact' if, instead of referring to this prophecy, she had mentioned the actual event of the sacrifice of the Paschal lamb in *Exodus* xii, 3–6; and had then proceeded to show how this was an allegory of the death of Christ. However, although she employs only a 'figure of thought' here, it does involve that concordance of Old with New Testaments and the further reference to the celestial Lamb of the Apocalypse, which constitutes the foundation of the 'allegory of the theologians'. Lines 803–4 and the whole of the following stanza provide the New Testament verification of this prophecy. In ll. 817 ff. the words of the second prophet to call Jesus by the title of 'Lamb' are considered; namely, those of St. John the Baptist. We are told, 'His wordeȝ acorded to Ysaye'[13]:

> ' "In Jerusalem, Jordan, and Galalye,
> Þer as baptysed þe goude Saynt Jon,
> His wordeȝ acorded to Ysaye,
> When Jesus con to hym warde gon,
> He sayde of hym þys professye:
> 'Lo, Godeȝ Lombe as trewe as ston,
> Þat dotȝ away þe synneȝ dryȝe
> Þat alle þys worlde hatȝ wroȝt vpon.
> Hymself ne wroȝt neuer ȝet non;
> Wheþer on hymself he con al clem.' " '

In ll. 829 ff. the maiden adds the anagogical sense to the two drophecies whose *sensus allegoricus* was expounded at ll. 805 ff.[14]:

' "In Jerusalem þus my lemman swete
Twyeȝ for lombe watȝ taken þare,
By trw recorde of ayþer prophete,
For mode so meke and al hys fare.
Þe þryde tyme is þerto ful mete,
In Apokalypeȝ wryten ful ȝare:
Inmydeȝ þe trone, þere saynteȝ sete,
Þe apostel John hym saȝ as bare ..." '

A true *allegoria in facto* is developed in ll. 919–24, where the dreamer – speaking in character as one who remains on the level of the *sensus litteralis*, 'þat leueȝ noþynk bot [he] hit syȝe' (l. 308) – remarks:

' "Þou telleȝ me of Jerusalem þe ryche ryalle,
Þer Dauid dere watȝ dyȝt on trone,
Bot by þyse holteȝ hit con not hone,
Bot in Judee hit is, þat noble note." '

It is particularly interesting that this *sensus litteralis* makes an explicit reference to the Old Testament. The maiden, who, as an inhabitant of the Kingdom of Heaven, looks at everything from the point of view of the *sensus spiritualis*, answers him by providing, first, a reference to the *sensus allegoricus*:

' "That mote þou meneȝ in Judy londe
. . . .
Þat is þe cyté þat þe Lombe con fonde
To soffer inne sore for maneȝ sake,
Þe olde Jerusalem to vnderstonde;
For þere þe olde gulte watȝ don to slake." '

(ll. 937–42)

The earthly Jerusalem is not seen by her as a town in 'Judee' where a mortal monarch reigned, but as the chosen altar where the Atonement was brought about. It is the *means* whereby man passes to his true goal, his real *patria*, the Heavenly Jerusalem – of which the earthly city is but a 'figure' or 'type'. She plays upon the traditional 'etymology' of the place-name – *visio pacis* – in order to make a *distinctio* that shows how the 'allegorical' and 'anagogical' senses of Jerusalem are related to each other as means and end respectively:

E

' "Of motes two to carpe clene,
And Jerusalem hyȝt boþe nawþeles –
Þat nys to yow no more to mene
Bot 'ceté of God', oþer 'syȝt of pes':
In þat on oure *pes watȝ mad at ene*;
Wyth payne to suffer þe Lombe hit chese;
In þat oþer is noȝt bot *pes to glene*
Þat ay schal laste wythouten reles." '

(ll. 949–56 – my italics)

(iii) THE FIGURE OF THE CHILD

In spite of the theologians' insistence that only the Bible was
capable of bearing a *sensus spiritualis*, it would not be surprising
if an educated poet, who had learnt to look for 'typological' or
'figural' significance in the narrative and the characters of the
Old Testament, acquired the habit of finding similar significance in other historical events or in his own experiences. It is
not unknown for poets to discern in retrospect some Providential
significance, or evidence of numinous guidance, in their own
experiences: the most familiar English example is Wordsworth's interpretation in the early books of *The Prelude* of
incidents from his childhood. The most famous medieval
example is, of course, Dante's reinterpretation of the idealizing
passion that he had felt for Beatrice from his ninth year on-
wards. This romantic passion had inspired him to write his
earliest verses – most of them being panegyrics of his lady in the
traditions of *fine amour* – which he anthologized and supplied
with a commentary in *Vita Nuova*. Some years after her death
he came to regard her as an incarnation of Divine revelation,
sent by God to direct him heavenwards; so it is appropriate
that in the *Commedia* she should act as his guide through the
heavenly region. In the present study I have already had occasion to compare the figure of the child in *Pearl* with that of
Beatrice in Dante's works. Just as most students of Dante have
recognized some ulterior significance behind the figure of
Beatrice, so some students of the English poem have suspected
that a deeper significance lies beneath the figure of the child.
Scholarship concerning the function of Beatrice is more
advanced, more discerning and better informed than most of
the discussions about the possible allegorical significance of the

characters in *Pearl*. So, in order to prepare the ground before considering the case of the child in *Pearl*, a very brief summary of the conclusions reached in recent years by some distinguished scholars about the meaning of Beatrice will be helpful.

There are two principal schools of thought about the significance of Beatrice in Dante's works. The first of these maintains that she is an allegorical figure to be understood according to the manner of the poets[15]: she is nothing more than a symbol of some abstract concept, such as Revelation, Faith, Theology or the supernatural life. We may state this opinion in another way by adopting the terminology that Aquinas employs in his discussion of poetic metaphor[16]: Dante is writing *literally* about such concepts as Revelation, Faith or Theology; but, instead of expressing them *proprie* (as the author of a theological treatise might have done), he presents them *figuratively* in the guise of the lady Beatrice. Those who uphold this view refuse to believe in the existence of a historical Beatrice and maintain that Bice Portinari has nothing to do with the case.[17]

But most modern scholars – including such distinguished medievalists as Erich Auerbach[18] and Étienne Gilson[19] – take a different view. They admit that when Dante introduces the figure of the 'donna gentile' in the *Convivio*, he is indeed following the 'method of the poets'; for he declares quite explicitly that this lady is not a real person, but only an allegory of Philosophy.[20] Beatrice, on the other hand, was a historical, Florentine girl who had inspired the lyrics of *Vita Nuova*. When Dante later (in the *Commedia*) transformed this living Muse into a 'type' or 'figure' of Divine Revelation, the 'typological' or 'figural' significance that she acquired existed *in addition to* the historical fact of her former life on Earth and her survival as a blessed spirit in Heaven – just as the *sensus spiritualis* of Scripture exists in addition to the literal-historical fact or event upon which it is founded.[21]

In the *Convivio* Dante is concerned with the wisdom that may be learnt from Philosophy, and not with the Christian revelation that is the province of Theology. It is not surprising, therefore, that such a work employs the kind of allegory that is concerned with the figurative representation of abstract concepts and ideas. But Dante came to realize that Philosophy, the abstract Logos, is insufficient to raise a man to Heaven; this can be accomplished only through the Word Incarnate – that is, through a historical process.[22] So it is fitting that the special act of Divine Revelation that is made for Dante's personal benefit should have been mediated through the living Beatrice; she is – in Auerbach's phrase – a 'figuration or incarnation of revelation',[23] not a mere conceptual symbol of revelation.

Like Beatrice, the child who is celebrated in *Pearl* really lived and died, and her soul – the author believes – is preserved in Heaven to await the resurrection of her body. This is what the figure of the child signifies literally; any 'spiritual' significance that she may carry will exist in addition to this literal-historical one. The poet claims that she revealed the fact of her salvation to him in a vision, just as Dante claims that Beatrice appeared to him after her death – in the case of *Pearl* it matters little whether we regard this claim as based upon actual experience or whether we consider it a poetic fiction that provides a suitable vehicle for the presentation of the author's beliefs about the child's fate after her death. There is one respect in which the presentation of the child in *Pearl* is more complicated than that of Beatrice in the *Commedia*: as we saw earlier in the present chapter,[24] the literal-historical narrative of the child's death and burial is not presented *proprie* – to employ Aquinas's terminology again – but figuratively as a fiction about a pearl that disappeared into the grass. But, as Aquinas remarks, such figurative presentation – an example of the 'allegory of the poets' – is part of the literal sense; what we are now concerned to discover is whether the child had for the poet any 'figural' meaning that exists in addition to her literal-historical significance.

It can be said without cynicism that it was fortunate for Dante that the girl whom he had adopted as his Muse died in time to become his personal intercessor in Heaven. Similarly, it may be said without flippancy that the English poet saw a particular significance for himself – as well as for the child – in the Providential 'timing' of the death of the human being who had monopolized all his affection. As already noticed, her death before she was two years old was, in the first place, an advantage to the child herself: by dying while still in a state of post-baptismal innocence she was able to pass immediately into the company of heavenly innocents and to become a bride of the Supreme Innocent. In Heaven she enjoys the fulfilment of what she had never ceased to pre-figure throughout her brief life on Earth.

In our examination of the argument of the debate we saw that the maiden teaches that the best hope of salvation for all men is through innocence; and she applies this to the particular case of the dreamer. The adult must be spiritually reborn and acquire the innocence and humility of a child if he would be admitted to the Kingdom of Heaven: the mourner's child is thus a 'type' or 'figure' of what he must himself become 'spiritually' in order to enter the Heavenly City. This lesson the author no doubt derived from meditating upon the beloved infant's death: there were available to him plenty of texts – in addition to the Gospel itself – that would have encouraged him to think in this 'tropological' way about the figure of a child.[25] But he appears to believe that the experience which inaugurated the lesson was Providential. Just as Dante believed that Beatrice was a living miracle – an incarnation of revelation – sent to Earth by God in order to attract him heavenwards, so the English poet appears to have believed that He sent this child to him as a privy agent for his love – whereas He sent His Son patently as a factor for the loves of all mankind – and withdrew her to Heaven in order to draw up his love after her. But He did more than that: by withdrawing her before she was two years old, He indicated 'typologically' the guise in which he must seek to pass through the gate into the Heavenly City. In this way the author extends the *solacium* of the *opportunitas mortis* to refer, not only to the advantages for the child, but also to the spiritual benefits that her early death has brought to her bereaved father.

In order to confirm that this is indeed how the poet regards the figure of the child, it is necessary to examine his use of the image of the pearl: which brings me to the second kind of allegory.

CHAPTER FIVE

The 'Allegory of the Poets'

The distinction between the 'allegory of the poets' and the 'allegory of the theologians' is sufficiently well known, though not always properly understood, by most students of medieval literature. Even more familiar is the fourfold division of the theologians' allegory; but it is not generally realized that the kind of allegory used by poets and the human authors of Scripture involves likewise several important subdivisions and distinctions.

We have already considered the views of Dante and of certain theologians on the interpretation of allegory; for a detailed discussion of the practical use of allegory we must look to classical and medieval treatises on rhetoric. In the present chapter the classical authority to whom I shall most often refer is Quintilian, because his *Institutio Oratoria* contains the most comprehensive, representative, lucid and sane discussion of the subject by a Latin author – though it is true that he did not influence medieval writers in as direct a manner as Cicero and the author of the *Rhetorica ad Herennium*. From among the rhetoricians of the Dark and Middle Ages I shall refer particularly to the encyclopaedists Isidore of Seville and Vincent of Beauvais, to the authors of the twelfth-century *Artes Poeticae*, and to Bede's *De Schematibus et Tropis Sacrae Scripturae*. The last mentioned work is of particular interest because of the way in which Bede's study of the literary style of texts originally written in Hebrew affects his taste and his precepts.

(i) ALLEGORY, PERSONIFICATION AND IRONY

Allegory and personification are nowadays commonly confused, because they frequently occur side by side; they often act in partnership and the one may even, in certain circumstances, be metamorphosed into the other. But for classical and medieval rhetoricians they were two distinct 'tropes' or 'figures of thought'.[1] Quintilian defines allegory as follows:

> 'Allegoria, quam inversionem interpretantur, aut aliud verbis aliud sensu ostendit, aut etiam interim contrarium. Primum fit genus plerumque *continuatis translationibus* . . .'[2]

He cites Horace, *Odes* I, xiv, as an example of this first *genus*:

> 'O Navis, referent in mare te novi
> fluctus . . . etc.'

– which continues the metaphor of the ship of state throughout the poem. As an example of allegory without metaphor, he cites Virgil, *Eclogues* ix, 7, where the only device is the author's disguising of his own identity in the figure of the shepherd, Menalcas. He also mentions *aenigma*, or 'riddle', as a variety of this figure; but the kind of allegory that is referred to in the words 'aut etiam interim contrarium' consists of the figure known as *irony*. Isidore[3] and Vincent of Beauvais[4] define allegory in much the same way as Quintilian: they likewise include irony as one of its variations – indeed, the association is made by Bede[5] and also by several of the Renaissance rhetoricians.

I shall discuss the definition of allegory as *translatio continuata* and the subdivision *aenigma* later in the present chapter. For the moment I confine my remarks to the statement that must surely come as a surprise to any modern reader who is unacquainted with ancient treatises on rhetoric: the assertion that irony is a species of allegory. It may seem to him that these rhetoricians were somewhat perverse in making irony a kind of allegory, while keeping personification as a completely distinct figure. I am not concerned here to decide whether or not their analysis of the relationships between these figures is altogether acceptable; but I believe that it affords the clearest possible demonstration of the essential characteristics of allegory as they understood it. If irony may be defined as 'saying one thing, but meaning the opposite of what you say', it is simply the extreme form of the principle that underlies all allegory: 'to say one thing, but mean something else'. An element of 'otherness', a veiling of intention or thought, is involved in the expression of it. It is true that to a limited extent personification likewise involves speaking of one thing in terms of another, in so far as an abstract concept or inanimate object is endowed with certain human faculties.[6] But these limitations are stringent and the device is a rigid one; allegory is a much more flexible figure.

The distinction between these two figures is not considered to be of much importance by modern scholars. All too often the terms 'allegory' and 'personification' (prosopopoeia) are used as if they were almost synonymous. The late Professor C. S. Lewis, for example, in an attempt to distinguish between 'symbolism' and allegory – a distinction which, incidentally, hardly coincides with that formulated by Gordon[7] – is concerned to show that allegory (i.e. the 'allegory of the poets') is nothing more than a figure of rhetoric. But much of his discussion of allegory is, in fact, concerned with personification. In particular he cites Dante's use of the figure of Amor in the sonnet from the *Vita Nuova* beginning: 'Io mi sentii svegliar dentro allo core.' He remarks that we might suppose that Love is here regarded as a Divinity, but he points out that Dante, in his commentary on the sonnet, makes it quite clear that it is merely a rhetorical figure, a personification of an abstract idea.[8] Now, Dante does not, in fact, name the figure that he here employs; but his description of it comes close to the definition of prosopopoeia by Isidore of Seville and does not resemble any medieval definition of allegory.[9]

The importance of the principle of 'otherness' upon which allegory is based cannot be overestimated. The interest of allegory often lies in the nature of the relationship between the thing or concept that is signified literally and the image by which it is figuratively represented; or – to adopt the useful terminology that I. A. Richards employs when treating of metaphor[10] – the relationship between the 'tenor' and its 'vehicle'. Sometimes the relationship is merely conventional or static; at other times it continually and subtly shifts or it introduces significant associations. The interplay of 'tenor' and 'vehicle' is most striking when the one is virtually opposed to the other: when, in fact, allegory involves irony.

A good example of this is afforded by the 'pardon' in *Piers Plowman*, B.vii. Langland's purpose in that episode is to discourage the belief that indulgences, which may be bought for cash, are effective passports to the Kingdom of Heaven. In opposition to this belief he sets up his ideal of Dowel as the only reliable guide to salvation. But he presents the situation allegorically: Truth (God) sends Piers a 'pardon'. When this document is unfolded, however, it is found to contain no declaration of indulgence, but simply the message: if you Do Well, you will go to Heaven; if you do evil, you will be consigned to the everlasting fire. So this 'pardon' is used ironically as a satirical instrument for questioning the value of official pardons. In Langland's allegory the 'vehicle' is diametrically opposed to the 'tenor'.

In *Pearl*, although the tension between 'tenor' and 'vehicle' never becomes as acute as in this example, the shifting relationship between the two is an important feature of its use of allegory and metaphor – especially in the development of the image of the pearl.

(ii) ALLEGORY AND METAPHOR

Whereas allegory was treated as a separate figure from personification, it was considered to be much closer to metaphor than it is usually acknowledged to be nowadays. In the eyes of many modern critics metaphor is hedged about with divinity, whereas allegory is a dog that must to kennel, in company with long-tailed simile; it must not be allowed through the hedge to foul the glades of the sacred wood of 'genuine' poetry.

It is no defence of allegory to recall its ancient definition as *translatio continuata*, and to argue that if metaphor is respectable, allegory must therefore be respectable too. For it will be retorted that the very process of 'extension' or 'continuation' involves deliberate manipulation and is always 'contrived' rather than generated; it is the product of topiary art rather than of vital propagation. The strength of the metaphor in Herrick's best known line – 'Gather ye rosebuds while ye may' – depends to a considerable extent upon the fact that the rosebuds cannot be precisely interpreted; their significance is not selectively delimited. They may symbolize the objects of youthful pleasure generally or youthful objects of amorous delight in particular; they may be just rosebuds. The *carpe diem* context reminds us that they will begin to wither almost as soon as they open out, and an insidious suggestion of the sadistic delight of enjoying something before its due season may also be present. Probably most modern critics would say that all these significations, and several other possibilities, are present in the metaphor.

Quite different is the image of the rosebud that is the object of the lover's quest in the *Roman de la Rose* and which symbolizes the lady's ultimate favour. This rosebud is attached to a rosebush which grows in a garden that is, in turn, situated in a walled park which contains, among other ornaments, a fountain at the bottom of which are two precious stones. Like the rosebud itself, all these objects have a fixed connotation and this may seem to drain all imaginative spontaneity and vitality out of the story.

It is no part of my present purpose to write an 'Apology for Allegory'. What I wish to establish for the purpose of the present study is that there are certain things which allegory (as defined by the rhetoricians) and metaphor have in common. For the remainder of this chapter I shall be concerned with a distinction that applies equally to both these figures – and, indeed, to any kind of symbolic expression.

In his discussion of 'parabolical poetry' – which he considers to be of 'higher character' than either narrative or dramatic poetry – Francis Bacon observes that allegory 'is of double use and serves for contrary purposes; for it serves for an infoldment; and it likewise serves for illustration'.[11] The distinction I shall be concerned with is between allegory – or symbolism or metaphor – which serves for concealment and that which serves for revelation. I shall examine the various modes of allegorical thought and expression that are ranged along the axis between the poles of what the rhetoricians call *aenigma* and what – for want of a better term – I propose to call 'apocalyptic' symbolism.

(iii) *Aenigma*

One of the subdivisions of allegory that Quintilian mentions is *aenigma* (VIII, vi, 52 and 53); but, because of his classical ideal of lucidity, he condemns it as a perverse form of the figure. Yet when Bede defines *aenigma* there is not a single word of condemnation. His definition reads simply: 'Aenigma est obscura sententia per occultam similitudinem rerum . . .' The reason for his tolerant attitude becomes apparent as soon as one looks at the illustrative example that he gives, which comes from Psalm lxviii, 13 (Authorized Version): 'the wings of a dove covered with silver, and her feathers with yellow gold'. He thinks that these words describe the eloquence of Scripture, full of Divine light; he finds other allegorical meanings for them as well.[12] Isidore likewise refrains from positively denouncing *aenigma*; he is content to distinguish it from *allegoria*, as follows:

'. . . Allegoriae vis gemina est et sub res alias aliud *figuraliter* indicat; aenigma vero sensus tantum obscurus est, et per quasdam imagines adumbratus . . .'[13]

No word of reproach appears in the twelfth-century *Artes Poeticae*. Matthew of Vendôme defines allegory thus: '. . . *allegoria* est alienum eloquium quando a verborum significatione dissidet intellectus'.[14] He gives the same illustrations of the figure as Isidore and simply defines *aenigma* in the following words: '. . . *aenigma* est sententiarum obscuritas quodam verborum involucro occultata'.[15] The example of Holy Scripture made *aenigma* respectable in the Middle Ages. Stimulated by Biblical precedent, medieval authors – including Dante, Langland and the author of *Pearl* – take a positive delight in introducing cryptograms, enigmatic allegories and 'dark conceits' into their own compositions.

The explanation that was usually given for the Scriptural use of *aenigma* was the desire of its authors to appeal to the ingenuity of learned readers and to avoid casting pearls before swine. Aquinas gives just such an explanation in his discussion of the Biblical use of metaphorical language[16] and a similar notion is expressed by Walter Hilton in *The Scale of Perfection*.[17] No doubt Dante deliberately emulates the practice of Holy Writ when he conceals the significance of the mysterious pageant in *Purgatorio* xxxiii under a cloak of enigmatic allegory and cryptic number symbolism. Similarly, Langland causes Patience at B.xiii, 151, to wrap up what is evidently meant to be a cardinal definition of 'Dowel' in such a knotty integument that scholars continue to argue about its interpretation.

More mundane considerations of practical prudence no doubt determined Langland's use of enigma in his prophecies at B.iii, 323–27, and viii, 151 ff. (if they have any meaning at all). Similar counsels of caution account for the fable of belling the cat in B. Prol. 146–209, which alludes to contemporary political events.[18] Sheer delight in describing one thing in terms of another is an important element in the Old English riddles; but this is also true of kennings, which do not purport to be enigmatical. Indeed, such delight in the ingenuity of 'translation' and in rendering one's meaning less obvious is often present in metaphorical expression, even when the writer is not attempting deliberately to conceal his meaning.

(iv) 'APOCALYPTIC' SYMBOLISM

At the opposite pole from *aenigma* stands the kind of allegory (or symbolism, or metaphor) where *A* is spoken of in terms of *B*, not out of any desire to conceal *A*, but because there is no other way of speaking of it: we are confronted here with genuine mystery rather than deliberate mystification. If *aenigma* is concerned to render the visible invisible, this kind of allegory is employed to make the invisible visible. Man can speak of God properly (*proprie*) only in negative terms. If he wishes to make positive statements about Him, it is absolutely necessary to employ symbolic, metaphorical or allegorical expression. So Aquinas in his discussion of the Biblical use of metaphor quotes from *The Celestial Hierarchy* by pseudo-Dionysius: 'Impossibile est nobis aliter lucere divinum radium, nisi varietate sacrorum velaminum circumvelatum.'[19] This kind of allegory occurs when we speak of the divine in terms of human attributes; of the heavenly in terms of the terrestrial; of the spiritual in terms of the material.

The designation which I employ to refer to this kind of allegory that serves to reveal rather than to conceal is 'apocalyptic' symbolism. The term is not entirely satisfactory, because in Modern English the word 'apocalyptic' is used to refer to the particular 'Apocalypse' or Revelation of St. John the Divine – and, by extension, to any chiliastic prophecy. I use the word in its etymological sense, in the common meaning of ἀποκαλύπτειν 'to uncover, reveal, disclose'. When I speak of 'apocalyptic' symbolism I mean any symbolic device that is used to make visible the divine and the supernatural phenomena of the 'other world'; I do not confine myself to the symbols and images that are peculiar to the Biblical *Apocalypse*, though some of these must occur frequently in any discussion of the use of this kind of symbolism in *Pearl*.

The principal advantage of this term is that it indicates that the device to which it refers is diametrically opposed to *aenigma*. This fact would not be indicated by other designations that might have been used, such as 'anagogical symbolism' or 'transcendental symbolism'. In any case, the first of these possible alternatives, besides being somewhat cacophonous, could easily lead to confusion with the theologians' *sensus anagogicus*. The kind of symbolism I am now discussing is related to that 'sense' in one respect (just as it is also related to the symbolism of the Platonists),[20] but differs from it in others.

What I mean by 'apocalyptic' symbolism can be most conveniently illustrated from Dante. The *Commedia* furnishes many examples of this kind of allegory or symbolism and enables us to see how it differs from *aenigma*, as well as how both are distinguished from the *sensus spiritualis* – or rather, Dante's counterpart to this mode of the theologians.

In Chapter Four we discussed the 'typological', 'figural' or 'spiritual' significance that Beatrice acquires in the *Commedia*. Here we are concerned with the *subiectum* of the poem merely in its literal sense, which is, according to the Epistle to Can Grande, 'the state of souls after death'. It will be remembered that Aquinas maintains that a poet's use of metaphor and allegory is contained within the literal sense; he also explains that this literal sense may be expressed either *proprie* or *figurative*.[21] Now, Dante is writing literally about disembodied souls who must wait until the General Resurrection to be reunited with their bodies. When he makes historical statements about their former lives on Earth he speaks about his characters *proprie*, but when he describes their condition in the other world he is compelled to speak *figurative*. In order to make these souls visible and audible to the reader he has to endow them with shadowless, 'spirit' bodies and to describe the punishments or rewards that they receive in physical terms. But these bodies do not really exist; they are a figurative device for rendering the invisible visible to us – just as when the human author of Scripture speaks of God's arm, but is really referring to His 'virtus operativa'.[22] What I wish to emphasize here, however, is that the figurative device that Dante inevitably employs is 'apocalyptic' symbolism. He employs the same device in the *Paradiso* when he distributes the various orders of beatified souls, whose real abode is in the timeless and extra-spatial 'realm' of

Eternity, among the spheres that constitute what the author of *The Cloud of Unknowing* calls 'ȝone bodely heuen, in whiche þe elementes ben fastnid'.[23] Even when, in the final cantos, Dante's vision penetrates the figurative veil of this 'bodely heuen', he cannot dispense with symbolism. He substitutes one metaphor for another: the 'bodely heuen' is replaced by the celestial rose.

Sometimes the figurative device that Dante employs in order to present the literal sense of his *subiectum* is not 'apocalyptic' symbolism but *aenigma*. This is true of such an episode as that of the Furies and Medusa, where interpretation is explicitly invited,[24] or of the pageant surrounding the gryphon, where some interpretation is obviously required if any sense is to be made of the passage.[25] These fabulous or chimerical figures are used to disguise a meaning that could have been expressed *proprie*, whereas the disembodied souls have to be presented as 'spirit' bodies because there is no other possible way of representing them.

The relationship between these two kinds of figurative representation and the way in which they differ from the 'figural' mode of expression mentioned in the last chapter are aptly illustrated in the figure of the child in *Pearl*. The poet speaks about her *proprie* when he communicates to us the biographical fact that she died before she was two years old. But he disguises her literal-historical identity figuratively when, in the opening stanzas, he refers to her, not as a child, but as a pearl.[26] The figurative device employed here is *aenigma*. During the account of the vision her disembodied soul appears to the dreamer as the visionary body of 'a mayden of menske, ful debonere'. Since this visionary body has no real existence, the poet is also speaking *figurative* here; but the figure he now employs is what I call 'apocalyptic' symbolism. Both these devices belong to the allegory of the poets and so, according to Aquinas's definition, are merely part of the literal sense: they are examples of what Augustine designates 'allegoria in verbis', not 'in facto'. However, I suggested in the last chapter[27] that the child may also have had for the poet a 'figural' significance that goes beyond the literal sense and corresponds in some respects to the theologians' 'allegoria in facto' which is a distinctive feature of their *sensus spiritualis*.

Often the symbolism that a poet uses of necessity to describe the other world is merely traditional and conventional; the commonest source for this kind of symbolism is the *Apocalypse*. This book was, however, regarded in different ways by different commentators and authors. Some looked upon it as a protracted *aenigma*, and offered various types of interpretation – religious, moral and even political. Other authors, however, do not bother with such interpretations, but simply treat the book as a source for 'machinery', 'furniture' or 'scenery' with which to provide an authoritative basis for their representations of Heaven. They regard it, appropriately enough, as a quarry for conventional 'apocalyptic' symbolism. That, indeed, is how the author of *Pearl* makes use of the book.

(v) AN INTERMEDIATE KIND OF ALLEGORY AND SYMBOLISM

Aenigma and 'apocalyptic' symbolism are, however, merely the two poles between which there extends a variety of allegorical and metaphorical modes, where it is neither the writer's intention deliberately to obscure his meaning nor, on the other hand, absolutely impossible for him to speak of his subject without resorting to symbolic and allegorical expression. With this kind of allegory and metaphor particularly, the interest lies in the interplay of 'vehicle' and 'tenor' that has already been mentioned.[28] Whether the relationship between the thing signified and the image or idea that signifies it consists of a happy congruity or a felicitous or catachrestical incongruity, it has the effect of making us look at the subject from an unusual or oblique point of view and of causing us to think in a new way about something that may be familiar or even commonplace.

Most instances of the poetic use of allegory fall within this intermediate category. The episode in *Piers Plowman*, B.vii, that I cited in order to demonstrate the relationship between allegory and irony, is of this type.[29] So is the final episode in the dream from *The Parlement of Foules* – the scene of the parliament of birds itself. Here Chaucer is really concerned with the attitudes towards love that are adopted by various classes of men, although he presents their views figuratively through the medium of a debate among different species of birds. But why does he bother to employ allegory at all? Would not a parliament of human lovers have served his purpose just as well? A proper critical appreciation of the poem must depend upon the answer to that question and upon our decision as to whether Chaucer is merely following literary precedents or whether there is some profounder and more intrinsic reason for his chosen mode of presentation.

This 'intermediate' kind of allegory or symbolism is a flexible mode of expression: one example of it may stand nearer the pole of *aenigma*, another nearer that of 'apocalyptic' symbolism. It is also possible that an example of allegory which, when regarded in its immediate context, must be classified as *aenigma* may, when considered in relation to the total context of the work in which it occurs, be seen to have the effect of concealing temporarily only in order to produce ultimately some deeper revelation. There is no more striking example in medieval literature of this paradox than that which is provided by *Pearl* itself.

CHAPTER SIX

The 'Allegory of the Poets' and the Interpretation of Pearl

(i) PERSONIFICATIONS AND POWERS

A few personifications and demi-personifications are mentioned in *Pearl*; but they disappear before we are able to scan their faces. The nearest the poet ever comes to animating any one of them is when, at ll. 130–1, he applies the feminine pronoun *ho* to Fortune. The most interesting feature about their behaviour is the way in which, as the poem advances, they give place to persons (allegorical and figurative, as well as 'real'). In the opening stanza, when the dreamer laments his loss of the pearl, he complains that he is 'fordolked of luf-daungere' – wounded to the quick by that power, familiar from the *Roman de la Rose* and other courtly love contexts, that is responsible for cutting the lover off from his beloved. Normally, this power is attributed to the lady herself, but here it is the severing power of death that has caused the separation – an imaginative extension of a commonplace idea.[1] Before the end of the poem, however, the mourner learns that the real agent who deprived him of the infant is nothing so superficial as a personified power from the realm of *fine amour*, but is indeed a personal God, Whom the narrator conceives of figuratively or allegorically as his Prince.

At l. 52, in the course of what amounts to a miniature *Psychomachia*, the narrator mentions the unsuccessful attempt of 'resoun' to propitiate him. Gordon remarks that the idea of reason stilling the passions is a commonplace and he sees no need to assume an echo of the *Roman de la Rose* here; he roundly denies that the word is a personification in this line.[2] But the fact that it occurs so soon after the allusion to *luf-daungere* may lead one to disagree with this opinion. It will be remembered that in Guillaume de Lorris's portion of the poem it is the lady Reason who attempts – also unsuccessfully – to console the lover after

F

Danger has expelled him from the rose-garden. That lady is not a personification of what we would call 'common sense', but represents rather the principle that is implanted in all men by God to direct them away from worldly distractions to the Divinity Himself. She has much in common with Boethius's Lady Philosophy; indeed, at l. 5659 of the Middle English translation she quotes from 'Boece of Consolacioun' the sentiment that 'in Erthe is not our countree'. But it is not only the abstract Reason who fails to console the mourner; even the more personal 'kynde of Kryst' seems too remote to have any effect upon him. It needs the lost child herself to bring the Christian consolation home to him. It is true that the maiden's function in the debate is similar in some respects to that of Boethius's Lady Philosophy and Guillaume's Lady Reason, whereas the impetuous and unstable dreamer may at times appear to behave almost like a personification of Wylle (cf. l. 56). It is possible that the idea of a contention between Reason and Will may have played some part in the genesis of the debate,[3] but the poem that was eventually produced gains immeasurably from the fact that the disputants are persons and not personifications.

At l. 98 the dreamer appears to believe that it is Fortune who conducts him through the marvellous landscape and in ll. 129–32 the continued *crescendo* of joy that he experiences seems to him to be characteristic of the unrestrained behaviour of that female power. Yet at l. 63 the narrator had remarked that his spirit was conveyed to the wondrous region 'in Godeʒ grace'. However, after the dreamer has been 'kaste of kytheʒ þat lasteʒ aye', he no longer has any illusions about the identity of the Prime Mover in this experience: his impetuous attempt to cross the stream 'watʒ not at my Prynceʒ paye'. When the maiden mentions Fortune she is careful to delimit that goddess's sphere of influence: 'þaʒ fortune dyd your flesch to dyʒe' – she remarks at l. 306 – God has promised to raise man up from the dead.

The maiden is also prepared to acknowledge the concept expressed by the term *wyrde*.[4] In ll. 274–5 she exclaims:

> ' "And þou hatʒ called þy wyrde a þef,
> Þat oʒt of noʒt hatʒ mad þe cler . . ." '[5]

– because it has converted the withering rose into an imperishable pearl. The maiden knows as well as does Lady Philosophy (in 'Boece of Consolacioun')[6] that *wyrde* – fate, destiny – is not an autonomous power, but merely the instrument of Divine Providence which disposes all things for the ultimate benefit of virtuous men; if only they could see the complete picture, they would realize this themselves. She does not mention God or His Providence by name here, because she is taking up the terminology the dreamer had used a few lines earlier. In the very first words he addressed to her he had complained of his lonely, miserable life apart from her, while she is enjoying herself in Paradise (ll. 241–48). Then he asked:

> ' "What wyrde hatȝ hyder my iuel vayned,
> And don me in þys del and gret daunger?" '
>
> (ll. 249–50)

By the end of the poem the mourner himself learns, as we have remarked, Who the real power behind the scenes is: it is no remote, personified abstraction or vaguely numinous power, such as *luf-daungere*, Fortune or *wyrde*, but an approachable Prince Whom he eventually acknowledges to be 'A God, a Lord, a frende ful fyin' (l. 1204).

The progress that the mourner makes during the action can be most readily measured by comparing the first speech he addresses to the maiden, which we have just been discussing, with the words of his final apostrophe of her after he has been sharply awakened from his vision:

> ' "O perle", quod I, "of rych renoun,
> So watȝ hit me dere þat þou con deme
> In þis veray avysyoun!
> If hit be ueray and soth sermoun
> Þat þou so stykeȝ in garlande gay,
> So wel is me in þys doel-doungoun
> Þat þou art to þat Prynseȝ paye." '   (ll. 1182–88)

The poet must have composed this second speech with the earlier one in mind. They both begin with the formal address ' "O perle", quod I', and in both speeches the mourner's situation in a sorrowful world is contrasted with the maiden's joyful status in Paradise. But there are significant differences. Instead of the unknown and rapacious 'wyrde' of l. 249 we find in l. 1188 the Prince Who is the pearl's rightful owner and the mourner's friend. Again, whereas in the earlier passage the mourner seemed to grudge the maiden her happiness, in the final apostrophe he rejoices in her lot, in spite of the fact that he remains in the 'doel-doungoun' of this earthly life. The compound *doel-doungoun* of l. 1187 is probably a deliberate verbal echo of l. 250: 'And don me in þys *del* and gret *daunger*'. The author may not have known that *daunger* and *doungoun* are etymologically related,[7] but he would have been aware of their phonetic and semantic relationships. In l. 250 the mourner is imprisoned in a state of frustration imposed upon him by his failure to appreciate the true situation; but in l. 1187 he recognizes that the only prison into which he has been cast is the prison of earthly life, where he must remain for a while in exile from his heavenly *patria*, the home of the Prince and of the transfigured child.

(ii)   STRANDS OF METAPHOR

We have seen that Quintilian defined the principal kind of allegory as 'translatio continuata'.[8] Most of the instances of *translatio continuata* in *Pearl* consist not so much of a metaphor extended into a continuous, consecutive narrative as of strands of metaphor that are woven into the poem's fabric, and which become visible only at certain places. So the effect is often one of broadcast or sporadic, rather than of continued, metaphor. One such metaphorical thread, that is too obvious for us to pursue through the length of the poem, results from the author's conceiving of the Kingdom of Heaven in terms of a medieval court and his thinking of Christ as a prince. The most important source of an extended metaphor is, of course, the parable of the pearl of great price. The function of the image of the pearl will be discussed separately at the end of this chapter. But this was not the only image that the parable yielded to the poet: it also provided the figure of the *negotiator* or 'merchantman' of *Matthew* xiii, 45, who is referred to as a 'jueler' at ll. 730 and 734. The poet applies the term metaphorically to the dreamer in the fifth stanza-group, where it acts as the link-word – except for those instances where he substitutes 'juel' in order to refer to the maiden. This application produces a crop of mercantile metaphors that have a bearing upon the passage about the

'forser' and the rose. The maiden reproves the dreamer for
being an incompetent 'jueler' who cannot recognize a bargain
when he sees one. The loss of the object that was so dear to him
is not worth mourning for; to do so is to waste time over an
ephemeral consideration: '[þou] busyeȝ þe aboute a raysoun
bref' (l. 268).[9] For the lost object was no jewel, but merely a
mortal rose. The 'wyrde', of which the dreamer had complained
at l. 249, is not a thief[10]: by securing what was formerly a rose
into His 'kyste', 'cofer' or 'forser', he has transformed it into a
'perle of prys'. This is almost like saying that by transferring it
to His bank He has transformed what was a rapidly diminishing
asset into a gilt-edged security:

> ' "Now þurȝ kynde of þe kyste þat hyt con close
> To a perle of prys hit is put in pref.
> And þou hatȝ called þy wyrde a þef,
> Þat oȝt of noȝt hatȝ mad þe cler;
> Þou blameȝ þe bote of þy meschef,
> Þou art no kynde jueler." '   (ll. 271–76)

Mercantile metaphors also appear in the next exchange
between the dreamer and the maiden. On learning that he may
not cross the stream to rejoin his lost beloved, the dreamer
exclaims:

> ' "My precios perle dotȝ me gret pyne.
> What serueȝ tresor, bot gareȝ men grete
> When he hit schal efte wyth teneȝ tyne?" ' (ll. 330–32)

In her reply the maiden reminds him that to complain against
God's will is unprofitable. As a result of being preoccupied with
grieving over minor losses men often miss something of greater
value:

> ' "For dyne of doel of lureȝ lesse
> Ofte mony mon forgos þe mo.
> Þe oȝte better þyseluen blesse,
> And loue ay God, in wele and wo,
> For anger gayneȝ þe not a cresse." '   (ll. 339–43)[11]

The metaphor is continued in the next stanza:

> ' "Þy mendeȝ mounteȝ not a myte,
> Þaȝ þou for sorȝe be neuer blyþe." '   (ll. 351–52)

The poet's use of the parable of the labourers in the vineyard might appear, in theory, to provide the clearest example of *translatio continuata* in the poem, especially as he follows it with what could be taken as an allegorical interpretation. But, in fact, his retelling of the story is most memorable for its naturalistic vividness. This can be heard in the vigorous colloquial rhythms of the workman's complaint – consisting entirely of simple, monosyllabic and disyllabic words until he brings his speech to an end by triumphantly producing the more learned term, 'counterfete'. It can be visualized in the lines that, unlike St. Matthew's narrative, follow the labourers into the vineyard after the conclusion of the wages negotiation and describe them at work:

> ' "Into acorde þay con declyne
> For a pené on a day, and forth þay gotʒ,
> Wryþen and worchen and don gret pyne,
> Keruen and caggen and man hit clos." '   (ll. 509–12)

The queue for payment referred to in l. 545 will probably be taken for granted by a twentieth-century Englishman, but the twentieth chapter of St. Matthew's Gospel knows nothing of it. The only possible example of the poet's adjusting the narrative in accordance with his particular interpretation occurs in l. 535, where those whom the lord finds unemployed at the eleventh hour are addressed as 'ʒemen ʒonge'.[12]

The truth is that the parable in St. Matthew's Gospel (like a number of the Gospel parables), although it may legitimately be regarded as allegory (in the broadest meaning of the term), is better considered as an *exemplum*, illustrating a principle of Divine Justice. The general principle has many possible applications; our poet applies it to the case of the child who dies soon after its baptism. The same is true of the parable of the pearl of great price: I shall argue later[13] that it is the principle which the whole parable illustrates that interests our poet more than particular allegorical or symbolical identifications of the image of the pearl. Nevertheless, the poet's use of this parable differs from his use of that of the labourers in the vineyard precisely because he does also use the image of the pearl to provide the basis for several subsidiary and local allegories; whereas the 'penny' is not put to such a multiplicity of uses.

In spite of the fact that the parable from *Matthew* xx and the poet's application of it to the case of the child constitute a fairly self-contained unit near the middle of the argument, it does make some contact with another part of the poem. When the labourers in the vineyard are first mentioned at l. 505 they are referred to as 'þys hyne' and the same word is applied to them at l. 632 in the course of the maiden's exposition of the parable. The only other use of the word in the poem is in its penultimate line:

> 'He gef vus to be his homly hyne
> Ande precious perleȝ vnto his pay.'   (ll. 1211–12)

As the mercantile metaphors, that we have noticed, are derived from the parable of the pearl of great price, so the metaphor of the servants may be derived from the other parable. There is, however, a significant difference between the 'hyne' who perform their part in the parable and the 'hyne' of this concluding prayer. The former were casual labourers, working for hire: the latter are '*homly* hyne', inmates of the Lord's household, whose principal desire is to serve Him in such a way as to please Him – syntactically 'vnto his pay' may be construed with 'hyne' as well as with 'perleȝ' – rather than to dispute the amount of the remuneration with which He 'pays' them. This reflects the general movement of the poem's argument from a mood of resentful aggrievement to one of resignation and a recognition that 'E'n la sua volontade è nostra pace'.

The change in the mourner's attitude is also emphasized by a verbal echo at the beginning of the final stanza, although there is no question of an extended metaphor here:

> 'To pay þe Prince oþer sete saȝte
> Hit is ful eþe to þe god Krystyin;'   (ll. 1201–2)

The phrase 'sete saȝte' occurs at only one other place in the poem; namely at l. 52, where the mourner describes how a desolating grief lurked in his heart 'þaȝ resoun sette myseluen saȝt', and goes on to describe how the consolation offered by 'kynde of Kryst' failed to pacify him. But by the time he reaches l. 1201 he is concerned with how he may satisfy Christ. A similar change in the mourner's response to the situation is reflected in the poet's handling of the image of the pearl.[14]

It may be objected that I am attaching too much importance

to a chance recurrence of the word 'hyne' and that I am attempting to join together improperly strands which the author has kept asunder. It will be pointed out that the parable of the vineyard is not employed to assuage the dreamer's rebellious grief at the loss of his pearl; on the contrary, it is intended to overthrow his objection to the maiden's enjoying in Heaven the full privileges of a queen rather than those of a mere countess – 'Oþer elleȝ a lady of lasse aray'. That is true; but there is no need to suppose that 'hyne' in l. 1211 is meant to summon up the whole of the context in which the parable occurred. It evokes only what the labourers and the dreamer have in common; namely, a selfish resentment of what God has ordained. In the course of the debate the dreamer learns, as do the labourers in the parable, that to complain about His decrees is unprofitable; it does not 'pay' – as the modern colloquial expression has it. His final petition shows that he has learnt true humility: he will be content if he is allowed to number himself among the Prince's domestic servants; he has no ambition for himself to be made an earl in His court – or even a lord 'of lasse aray'.[15]

These examples of extended metaphor, derived from Biblical parables, are distributed in a desultory fashion throughout the poem. All the more concentrated and more coherent examples of *translatio continuata* belong to the category of *aenigma*, which is the subject of the next section.

(iii)   DARK CONCEITS
The author's use of the image of the pearl has been interpreted by more than one scholar as if it were an example of a continuous *aenigma*; others have treated the whole poem as if it were an *aenigma*. The best known example of the former approach is Schofield's interpretation of the pearl as symbolizing 'clean maidenhood'[16]; the most highly developed instance of the latter approach is Sister Madeleva's thesis that the poem is a study in the condition known to religious as 'spiritual dryness'.[17] More recent scholars, such as Wellek[18] and Gordon,[19] have had no difficulty in exposing the crudity of these approaches and in demonstrating that the interpretations are grossly oversimplified. But in their eagerness to undermine the arguments of those who regard the poem as 'total allegory',

they have tended to underestimate the importance of the part that *aenigma* does play. It amounts to something more than 'minor allegories'[20] and incidental metaphors: there are threads of *aenigma* woven into the whole length of the poem's fabric. To fail to recognize their presence is to fail to appreciate an important and characteristic aspect of this poet's art and to run the risk of misunderstanding his argument.

In the poem's opening stanzas the mourner presents in a figurative guise the literal-historical events of his loss of the baby girl through death and of his visit to her grave-plot. The figurative representation of these events takes the form of an enigmatic narrative about his loss of a pearl, which slipped into the grass, and of the narrator's visit one August day to the spot where this happened. The spot is not described as if it were a graveyard: it is a beautiful 'erber grene' where 'spyceʒ' have now sprung up. It has affinities with the kind of idyllic land-scape that provides the setting for many a medieval poetic vision; so it is not surprising that the narrator goes on to tell how, overpowered by the fragrance of the 'spyceʒ', he fell into the slumber that brought him the vision.

One of the most interesting features of any allegory is the relationship between the 'tenor' and the 'vehicle'.[21] In the latter part of this initial *aenigma* it is difficult to say which is the more fundamental: the 'historical' visit to the child's grave-plot is presented figuratively as the mourner's entry into an orna-mental plesaunce which blossoms into symbols and 'conceits'. The reason for this curious mode of representation is that the poet wishes to hint darkly at the 'fruits' of the maiden's death which are to be indicated in a more explicit manner during the account of the vision.[22]

It is therefore appropriate that, as soon as the account of the vision begins, this enigmatical mode is abandoned and another kind of symbolism takes its place. While the mourner is awake and conscious of his earthly surroundings his perception is clouded and he can see eternal truths only through a haze obscurely, but in the vision he is enabled to see them face to face. So it is fitting that *aenigma* is employed in the introductory stanzas and that the vision is conveyed to the reader by means of the 'apocalyptic' symbolism that will be discussed in the next section.

Nevertheless, certain strands of the introductory *aenigma* are perpetuated throughout the account of the vision, though for most of the time they are concealed, being woven into the 'seamy side' of the tapestry, as it were, and appearing on the surface of the design only at a few selected points.

The *aenigma* in the opening stanzas is remarkably complex, sophisticated and 'conceited'.[23] When a fourteenth-century reader saw the first eight lines of the poem for the first time, he would have supposed that he was about to read a verse lapidary; for these lines contain several of the stock phrases and conventional formulas of that *genre*. Three of them appear in the first two lines[24]:

> 'Perle, plesaunte to prynces paye
> To clanly clos in golde so clere . . .'[25]

In the first place, it was customary that each set of verses in the lapidary should have as its first word the name of the precious stone that was to be discussed. Secondly, it was not unusual to declare that such a gem was worthy to be the prized possession of a king or prince. Finally, there was often a reference to the proper setting for the gem; in almost every instance, gold was considered to be the ideal setting. Only when he reached the 'Allas!' at the beginning of l. 9 would the original reader have realized that this was no ordinary lapidary. The alternation of the feminine and neuter pronominal forms, *her* and *hit*, may have caused him to suspect that the pearl was a symbol for a human being.[26] The mention of *luf-daungere* in l. 11 would help to confirm the reader's suspicions about the human identity of the lost pearl; but, at the same time, it would probably have misled him into identifying the human being with a lost mistress rather than a lost baby girl.

The author uses the lapidary formulas in the manner of a rhetorical 'topic' – a point of departure for his argument that would be familiar to his readers.[27] He evidently expected them to recognize the peculiar literary *genre* to which the eight opening lines belong so that they might appreciate the 'conceits' which, later in the poem, are developed from these stereotyped phrases. It has often been noticed that l. 6 (which, however, does not consist of one of the regular lapidary formulas) is echoed later in the poem. At l. 6 the words 'So smal, so smoþe her sydez were' describe the material gem: at l. 190 they are adapted to the description of the maiden whom the pearl represents figuratively: 'So smoþe, so smal, so seme slyzt'. Another obvious example of such a 'conceit' (which does involve a regular lapidary formula) occurs at l. 1188, where the first line of the poem is recapitulated, but with a specific allegorical meaning: having learnt from his vision that the lost child has become a bride of Christ, the dreamer rejoices in the knowledge that his pearl (whom he had once selfishly regarded as his own property) is now 'to þat Prynsez paye'. The use of the familiar lapidary formula helps to emphasize the fact that Christ, and not the dreamer, has always been the pearl's rightful owner.

It is perhaps not so obvious that the conventional allusion, in l. 2, to the ideal setting for the pearl is also worked into the allegory. There is no verbal recapitulation of this line, but the relationship between the pearl and its setting becomes a theme of some importance, which is developed allegorically as the poem proceeds. The development begins in the second stanza of the poem, where the author is speaking allegorically of the child's death and burial. He laments that his pearl lies in the ground, covered with earth; he mourns 'hir color so clad in clot' (when it should be set 'in golde so clere'). In ll. 23–24 he reproaches this unworthy and unsympathetic 'setting':

'O moul, þou marrez a myry iuele,
My priuy perle wythouten spotte.'

In the course of his dream, the maiden tells him that he is mistaken in thinking in this way about the fate of his pearl, for she is, in reality, safely locked up in a 'cofer' or 'forser'; namely, the 'gardyn gracios gaye' of Paradise.[28] Yet a pearl that is locked away in a treasure-chest cannot be said to be displayed in its ideal setting. However, this is only an intermediate stage in the development of the metaphor. At ll. 917 ff. the dreamer asks the maiden whether there are 'no wonez in castel-walle', no 'gret cité', where she, and the other brides of the Lamb, have their abode. For – as he remarks –

' "So cumly a pakke of joly iuele
Wer euel don schulde lyz þeroute." '   (ll. 929–30)

The maiden responds to this question by directing him to a

place from which he can see the New Jerusalem. It is significant that, in the description of the Heavenly City that follows, emphasis is placed upon gold and light, thus providing a background against which the immaculate whiteness of the maiden and her pearl-adorned companions shows up to advantage. It seems that the pearl has indeed been placed in a setting of 'golde so clere'.

But at this point the author does not make any *explicit* reference to the metaphor of the proper setting for the pearl; the maiden is presented simply as 'my lyttel quene . . . þat watȝ so quyt' (ll. 1147-50). The actual announcement that the pearl has been placed in a setting which the dreamer evidently regards as ideal for her is postponed until l. 1186, where, reflecting upon what has just been revealed to him in his 'veray avysyoun', he rejoices in the knowledge that she 'so stykeȝ in garlande gay'. As already noticed,[29] there may be an allusion here to the iconographical symbolism of a particular kind of *garlande*: a golden *corona*, which, in the ecclesiastical art of the time, symbolized the New Jerusalem. The pearls and gems that were set in these *coronae* represented the blessed inhabitants of the Heavenly City. This iconographical commonplace provides the poet with an apt and felicitous way of translating the sublime subject of the description, which concluded the vision, into terms of the simple, Lapidary formula from l. 2. It is appropriate that this should occur in the final stanza-group, where the 'link-word' and refrain are supplied by a recapitulation of the Lapidary formula from l. 1.

The Lapidary is not the only source of the 'conceits' in the opening *aenigma*: the poet has culled another crop of them from the herbal. At the beginning of the third stanza the narrator tells how 'spyces' sprang up from the place where the pearl had slipped away from him into the grass. But by the end of the stanza he seems to be saying that the spices sprang from the pearl itself.[30] By this time the original reader would probably have realized that the image of the pearl is being used to disguise the identity of a deceased human being. But he would have found the spices that spring from it a little more puzzling. They presumably represent plants growing on the grave-plot, but the representation is hardly naturalistic, because the herbs that are named in the next stanza could not possibly have been

found flourishing together in England – and at the same season
of the year. Gordon[31] remarks pertinently that spices were considered to be the most precious of plants. No doubt the poet is
chiefly concerned to assemble the most precious plants he
knows of, for only they are fit to spring from the spot 'þer such
rycheȝ to rot is runne'. A further example of the poet's licence
is the fancy that these spices have sprung spontaneously from
the buried corpse.[32] It is appropriate that such spices, rather
than violets or other meadow-plants, should spring from the
grave-plot of a virgin who was as sweet and precious as any of
them.

Preciousness is not the only symbolic association carried by
these spice-plants. Flowers are regarded universally as symbols
of resurrection; strictly speaking, of the resurrection of the body
but, by association, they also symbolize the survival after death
of the soul. This symbolism was particularly popular in the
Middle Ages.[33] We have already seen that the Biblical metaphor
in ll. 31–32 was a common 'topic' of Christian consolation,
used to assure the bereaved of the resurrection of the deceased.[34]

But the herbs on the maiden's grave-plot symbolize something
more than the fact that she flourishes in another 'gardyn
gracios gaye'. They have medicinal properties that exert a
spiritual effect upon the mourner: their scent overcomes him
and induces the sleep that brings the healing vision.[35]

In l. 32 the notion of 'harvest home' is grafted on to the main
Biblical allusion (i.e. *John* xii, 24)[36] and is continued in the next
stanza, where the poet tells how he visited the grave-plot 'in a
hyȝ seysoun' in August, the month 'Quen corne is coruen wyth
crokeȝ kene'. Authors of dream poems often give the date when
their vision was supposed to have come to them.[37] The dating
of the vision in *Pearl* may be autobiographical, or symbolic, or
both. The 'hyȝ seysoun' referred to here is the highest ecclesiastical feast of the month of August; namely, the Assumption
of the Virgin Mary celebrated on August 15th. There is propriety in the poet's naming this day, when the entry of the
Queen of Heaven into her kingdom is celebrated, as the day
when he was vouchsafed the vision that informed him that his
own 'lyttel quene' had come into her inheritance in that realm.
Though I do not share Gordon's opinion that the 'hyȝ seysoun'
is Lammas, I agree with him that there may be in these lines a

symbolic allusion to 'the gathering of the Lord's harvest, with the pearl as one of the "first-fruits"; cf. 894'.[38] It is the whole month of August, and not just the single day of Lammas, that provides the almost inevitable cue for mentioning the action of reaping. The poet is alluding to the traditional 'occupations of the months' – an iconographical commonplace in medieval miniatures, sculptures and stained glass.[39] The modern reader may think that even August is a little early for the grain harvest in the north-west Midlands, but this date is less astonishing than the one mentioned by the thirteenth-century encyclopaedist Bartholomew the Englishman in his *De Proprietatibus Rerum*. The relevant passage is translated by Trevisa thus (Book IX, chap. xv):

> 'Julius is paynted with an hoke repynge corne: for then is couenable repynge tyme . . .'[40]

According to Bartholomew, August is the month for threshing. The reason for this may be that he is following a southern European tradition. The one which our poet follows is more northerly, but it is stereotyped, nevertheless. We have already seen that in the opening *aenigma* symbolism and tradition count for more than ecological accuracy.

There are yet other possible 'conceits' to be noticed in the opening stanzas. We have seen how the poet introduces into the third stanza the fanciful notion that spices spring from the buried corpse of the lost pearl. In ll. 33–36 the dead child is, in fact, referred to as both a pearl and a seed. I would suggest tentatively that this equation of pearl and seed may even involve a play upon the meaning of *grayneʒ* in l. 31. Because of the Scriptural allusion in this line the primary meaning of the word must be 'seed of corn': *OED* cites this instance from *Pearl* as the earliest recorded example of *Grain*, sb.[1] 1: 'A single seed of a plant, esp. one which is small, hard and roundish in form'. But it is interesting that the dictionary gives the following definition for *Grain*, sb.[1] 6: 'A bead, esp. one of the beads of the rosary (so F. *grain*); also, a pearl. *Obs*'. The earliest example of this sense cited by *OED* is from one of the lyrics in MS. Harley 2253:

> 'A wayle whyte ase whalles bon,
> a grein in golde that godly shon.'[41]

Professor Brook glosses *grein* in the lyric as 'bead of a rosary'. However, since the *grein* is white, and since pearls could be used as rosary beads, it is very probably a pearl that is intended here. This would appear to be a rare use of the word,[42] but *Pearl* is full of rare words and of more common words used in uncommon senses. It is interesting that the word should be used in this sense in this particular lyric. Like *Pearl* it employs rhyme and alliteration; it also uses the common alliterative 'tag': 'whyt ase whalles bon' – which occurs in *Pearl* in a modified form at l. 212. Most interesting, however, is the similarity between the second line of the lyric and the second line of *Pearl*. In both poems there is an allusion to the lapidary formula that mentions the ideal setting for the gem as gold. Again, in the lyric the white *grein*, that is placed in that setting, refers figuratively to a woman – just as the pearl does in our poem. This secular lyric is indeed just the kind of poem that we might expect the author of *Pearl* to have known.

The suggested play upon the meaning of *grayneȝ* would seem far-fetched, were it not for the fact that there are a number of examples of verbal play in the poem; the author evidently took delight in this kind of virtuosity. There is also other evidence to suggest that he is making a fanciful equation of pearl and seed. At ll. 43–44 he lists the *worteȝ*, which are presumably to be identified with the *spryngande spyceȝ* of the previous stanza. It is significant that one of them is the *gromylyoun* – or gromwell. Gollancz remarks: 'It is noteworthy that in the Middle Ages it was believed that the seed of the gromwell resembled a pearl in form'[43]; but he does not indicate his authority for this assertion. However, *MED* (under *gromil*) quotes statements from two ME herbals – *Agnus Castus* and the translation of *Macer Floridus de viribus herbarum* – that it has a white seed like a pearl. In any case, the hard, white, oval, marble-like seed of the gromwell (*Lithospermum*) might be expected to remind anyone who saw it of a pearl, whether he lived in the fourteenth or the twentieth century.

In an article on 'The Author of *Pearl* as a Herbalist'[44] E. Wintermute notices that one of the species of gromwell, the *Lithospermum officinale* – we have already mentioned the medicinal properties of the 'spyceȝ' in *Pearl* – bears the 'vulgar' name *herbe aux perles*. But he derives his information from the *Diction-*

naire De Botanique by Henri Baillon,[45] who gives no indication of the antiquity of this name, although it would seem to be pre-Linnaean. I have not been able to trace the name itself back as far as the fourteenth century; but I have found it recorded as early as Cotgrave's *Dictionarie of the French and English tongues* (1611). Under the article on Fr. *perle* Cotgrave gives as the English equivalent of *herbe aux perles* the following: *pearle-plant*; *lichwall*; *gromell*. Again, in the article on *herbe*, it is rendered: *perle-plant*; *lich-wall*; *grommill*; *gremill*.[46] This popular name for the plant is, no doubt, much older than the early seventeenth century and, in view of the descriptions in the ME herbals, it is not impossible that it was current even in the time of our poet.

(iv)   THE REPRESENTATION OF THE VISION

The introductory stanzas may be likened to a theatre curtain, specially designed for a particular production, that is covered with symbols which hint somewhat enigmatically at the principal themes of the drama that is to be enacted on the stage. At the beginning of the account of the vision the curtain is raised and the action proceeds, for most of the time, in a manner that is immediately intelligible. However, as the action is concerned with the revelation of heavenly mysteries, the poet inevitably employs what I have described as 'apocalyptic' symbolism – the kind of symbolism or allegory that makes visible the invisible and represents spiritual truths in terms of material imagery. The child's beatified soul appears in the guise of a 'mayden of menske ful debonere' with a body of adult stature, in spite of the fact that, in reality, her body has not yet been resurrected. She is still described as a pearl throughout the vision, but this description is used merely as a metaphorical epithet or title; it is no longer the sole means of referring to her and so it no longer disguises her identity.

One of the features of 'apocalyptic' symbolism is that it relies to a large extent upon conventions and traditions; another is that it does not insist on continual interpretation of detail. This is true, not only of the presentation of the former child's beatified soul, but also of most of the details of the description of the heavenly region. The description of the New Jerusalem follows fairly faithfully the account in *Revelation*. It includes the catalogue of precious stones that constitute the foundation of the Heavenly City; but the poet refrains from giving an allegorical interpretation of them in the manner of the medieval lapidaries.[47] Indeed, the few modifications of the original that he does make move away from the allegorical towards 'naturalistic' description: he adds certain details that show that he thinks of the New Jerusalem in terms of a medieval city.[48] This makes the heavenly phenomena seem more familiar and increases the illusion of seeing celestial truths 'face to face'.

The description of the marvellous landscape, with which the account of the vision begins, is rather more interesting, because the poet has more freedom to indulge his fancy. Although he draws on traditional material,[49] he is not tied so closely to the letter of an authoritative text as he is when he describes the New Jerusalem. The difference between this landscape and earthly landscapes is one of degree rather than of kind. Indeed, the narrator would appear to say as much himself, if one takes his statement literally that

> '. . . vrþely herte myȝt not suffyse
> To þe tenþe dole of þo gladneȝ glade.'   (ll. 135–36)

What we are presented with is a fairly ordinary terrestrial scene upon which a kind of alchemical transmutation has been effected; precious materials are substituted for base matter. What impresses us most vividly, however, is that Art has taken over from Nature. Tree-trunks are 'as blwe as ble of Ynde' (a colour from the paintbox, not from Nature) and their leaves are 'As bornyest syluer'. The river-banks gleam 'As fyldor fyn', the pebbles at the bottom of the stream are precious stones that cause the water to glow; even the gravel that scrunches underfoot consists of 'precious perleȝ of oryente'. The bird-song is not compared with that of earthly blackbirds or thrushes, but is said to be superior to the sounds made by 'sytole-stryng and gyternere'. When he wants a simile to describe the effect of the submerged jewels shining through the water, he thinks of 'glente þurȝ glas þat glowed and glyȝt' (that is, ecclesiastical stained glass), and his impulse, when first confronted with the landscape, is to compare its ornamentation to a tapestry:

> 'For wern neuer webbeȝ þat wyȝeȝ weuen
> Of half so dere adubbemente.'   (ll. 71–72)

G

Nothing emphasizes more strongly the fact that the poet thinks of the landscape as the work of an artist than the use of 'adubbemente' and 'dubbed' as the link-words throughout this stanza-group.

Some modern readers may deplore the subjugation of Nature to such a gaudily ornate kind of art. So they may take comfort from the fact that the details of this landscape are not meant to be taken *proprie* (to adopt Aquinas's terminology) but *figurative*: the poet is literally concerned with representing the preciousness of a transcendent, spiritual realm. Yet even the most committed Wordsworthian will probably admit the imaginative power of one simile that occurs in this passage. We have already mentioned one of the similes that is applied to the submerged precious stones, but it acts in conjunction with another:

> 'In þe founce þer stonden stoneʒ stepe,
> As glente þurʒ glas þat glowed and glyʒt,
> As stremande sterneʒ, quen stroþe-men slepe,
> Staren in welkyn in wynter nyʒt . . .'   (ll. 113–16)

So this region, where it is (presumably) perpetual spring, even contains its counterpart to the shimmering of stars in the frosty night-sky – but without the attendant disadvantages of darkness and cold, or the encumbrance of sleep, which prevents men on Earth from fully enjoying the beauty that shines above their heads. By placing this splendour below the dreamer's feet, the poet causes the most exalted of spectacles that is visible from Earth to appear in the lowliest position in this realm of transcendent beauty. This simile taken from Nature is all the more effective for occurring in a passage where Art predominates over Nature.

The other most memorable simile in the poem occurs in the description of the New Jerusalem. Like the one we have just considered, it is drawn from Nature and – as befits the ancillary function of a simile – is in a different key from the 'apocalyptic' symbolism that is the characteristic mode of these descriptions:

> 'Ryʒt as þe maynful mone con rys
> Er þenne þe day-glem dryue al doun,
> So sodanly on a wonder wyse
> I watʒ war of a prosessyoun.'   (ll. 1093–96)

The aptness of this simile for describing the dreamer's sudden awareness of the presence of the heavenly assembly – the city 'watȝ sodenly ful wythouten sommoun' – recalls the precision of imagination that is to be seen in some of Dante's similes. The fact that it is not in the same 'key' as the dominant mode of the imagery in the context will be appreciated if one looks at the preceding stanza-group where 'mone' is employed as the link-word, but for a negative purpose:

> 'The mone may þerof acroche no myȝte;
> To spotty ho is, of body to grym,
> And also þer ne is neuer nyȝt.
> What schulde þe mone þer compas clym
> And to euen wyth þat worþly lyȝt
> Þat schyneȝ vpon þe brokeȝ brym?
> Þe planeteȝ arn in to pouer a plyȝt,
> And þe self sunne ful fer to dym.'   (ll. 1069–76)

That was 'scientific' fact; the New Jerusalem was thought to be situated beyond the Primum Mobile, and so was far beyond the sphere of the moon. The New Jerusalem is a spiritual region where the physical light of Sun and Moon are not needed, because

> 'Þe self God watȝ her lombe-lyȝt,
> Þe Lombe her lantyrne, wythouten drede.'
>   (ll. 1046–47)

To attempt to establish precisely the location of the marvellous landscape would be a vain and misleading exercise. It seems best to suppose no more than that it is a visionary landscape in a personal dream, where contact between the Earthly and Heavenly is made. The further side of the stream affords a place where the New Jerusalem may alight (ll. 981–88) and the near side a vantage point from which a dreaming mortal may survey it. The sundering stream certainly represents the severing power of death. But it does not *demand* to be interpreted in the same way that the enigmatic symbolism of the opening stanzas does; so it may qualify as an example of 'apocalyptic' symbolism. Much the same is true of the only other important item of 'apocalyptic' symbolism that can be given a precise symbolic interpretation; namely, the maiden's dress. I shall argue later that it signifies the virtues and graces that entitle her to the particular status that she enjoys in the heavenly kingdom. But that is as much a question of decorum as of allegory; it would have been inappropriate for her to be dressed in any other manner. Indeed, in the Middle Ages, when a person's dress was commonly an indication of his social status or his profession, such a detail would probably have been attributed to the poet's desire to achieve verisimilitude rather than to any intention to construct an allegory.

(v) THE FUNCTION AND MEANING OF THE IMAGE OF THE PEARL

The image of the pearl acts as a loadstone that draws together the various objects and concepts to which it is applied and relates them all to the poem's *thema*[50]: the parable of the pearl of great price. Its various applications involve metaphorical modes or allegorical devices that are ranged along the whole extent of the axis between *aenigma* and 'apocalyptic' symbolism. We have seen how it is used in the *aenigma* at the beginning of the poem. Its occurrences as 'apocalyptic' symbolism are mostly ornamental and incidental: for example, the pearls that adorn the maiden's attire or those that are substituted for gravel and which scrunch underfoot as the dreamer walks through the paradisial landscape. Such ornamental uses help to keep the poem's dominant image constantly in the reader's mind.

Most of the primary applications of the image belong to that intermediate range of metaphorical modes where the changing relationships between 'tenor' and 'vehicle' provide the main interest. The principal applications of the image include: the child, whose loss the narrator mourns, and her blessed spirit in heaven; the Kingdom of Heaven itself; that which the narrator prays we may all become in order to please the Prince. It should also be remembered that the Lamb Himself and all the maidens in the heavenly procession are described as jewels. Presumably, the same metaphorical image is applied to all of them because they have something in common. So, in order to understand the meaning of the image of the pearl, it is necessary to discover how these objects are interrelated and why the relationship is expressed through that particular image.

One reason for choosing a pearl as the image to express the common relationship is that in the fourteenth century it could have been applied with propriety to any of the objects I have listed; there were precedents for each one of these applications – whether in the Scriptures, in saints' legends, in secular lyrics and romances, or in art.[51] But the main reason must be sought in the *sentence* of the parable that the author adopts as his *thema*. The parable in *Matthew* xiii, 45–46 is concerned explicitly with the Kingdom of Heaven. But so are several other parables in the Gospel: it is therefore necessary to ask what is distinctive about this one. The parable makes the points that the pearl is unique and that it is supreme: it is the one object of supreme value, to obtain which the merchant is content to sacrifice all his possessions; it has monopolized his desires. Translated into philosophical or theological terms, what the parable exemplifies is the principle of the *summum bonum*.[52] This is also the primary signification of the image of the pearl in the poem. But besides representing the concept itself, the pearl is applied to beings who participate in the Sovereign Good and in whom it is reflected, as well as to objects that are associated with it, that betoken it or proclaim it. This signification indicates the nature of the relationship between the various objects to which the poet applies the image.

The importance in the argument of *Pearl* of the concept of the *summum bonum* has been noticed by John Conley.[53] He is mainly concerned to show how the poem's meaning may be illuminated by one of the principal arguments in Boethius's *Consolation of Philosophy*, where this concept is of fundamental importance. But, long before Boethius wrote the *Consolation*, the idea of the *summum bonum* was implicitly stated in the parable of the pearl of great price. The primary significance that the image of the pearl had for the poet can thus be found in the Gospel parable without having recourse to any gloss or commentary: the poet has read the parable 'With the same Spirit that its Author *writ*'.[54] Moreover, in spite of the importance of the concept of the *summum bonum* in *Pearl*, and despite certain other similarities that I have mentioned when discussing the poet's use of personifications,[55] the poem's argument is not quite as close to that of Boethius as Conley would have us believe.

In the *De Consolatione Philosophiae*, Lady Philosophy begins her discussion of the *summum bonum* from the premise that what men most desire is happiness (*beatitudo*); but she distinguishes between true happiness and false felicity. The latter consists of delight in the temporal goods that men most desire, including wealth, power, fame and pleasure. It is interesting to see that under the last of these (*voluptas, iucunditas*) she lists the delight that man has in his wife and children (Lib. III, Prosa ii). But these are only partial, contingent, mutable and corruptible objects of happiness, subject to the vicissitudes of Fortune. In order to achieve true happiness man must attain to the enjoyment of the perfect, indivisible, immutable and eternal good, the Supreme Good, which is beyond the power of Fortune and which Lady Philosophy identifies with God Himself (Lib. III, Prosa ix).

Conley applies Lady Philosophy's argument to *Pearl* thus:

> 'The theme of *Pearl*, as of *The Consolation*, might be called the sovereign theme of the Christian tradition, as of life itself: the nature of happiness, specifically false and true happiness. Like the Boethius of *The Consolation*, as well as like St. Augustine of *The Confessions* and Troilus of *Troilus and Criseyde*, the narrator of *Pearl* had mistaken true for false happiness. In losing his pearl,
>
> "Þat er watȝ grounde of alle my blysse . . ."   (l. 372)
>
> he had lost his happiness. When the virgin informs him, in a beautiful superimposed metaphor, that what he has lost "was but a rose"
>
> "Þat flowred and fayled as kynde [nature] hyt gef,"
>   (l. 270)
>
> the lost pearl is plainly identified as a transient, therefore, in the language of *The Consolation*, as an imperfect good. In Boethian symbolism, which is also to say, in medieval symbolism, the lost pearl is another lost Eurydice . . .'

Conley then quotes from the famous twelfth metre of Boethius's third book, which retells the story of Orpheus's fatal backward glance and adds a *moralitas*. He also quotes from the Chaucerian translation, which embodies certain glosses on the passage, and then he adds the following comment:

> 'Plainly, if Eurydice is to be viewed as one of the "lowe thinges of the erthe", then immunity should not be imputed to an infant.'[56]

It is not clear what Conley understands by the 'pearl'. Does he identify it with the happiness that the narrator had derived from his love for the infant or with the infant herself? The last sentence quoted suggests that he intends the latter. But, whichever he intends, my criticism of his reading of the poem is unaffected: nowhere in the poem is the pearl identified as a 'transient' or 'imperfect good'; the image of the pearl represents throughout the poem the Supreme Good – or things associated with it, or that will conduct us to it. Conley's error seems to derive from a misunderstanding of the maiden's first speech. What she says, in fact, is that *if* the mourner must lose his happiness on account of a gem that was dear to him,

> ' "Me þynk þe put in a mad porpose,
> And busyeʒ þe aboute a raysoun bref . . ." '   (ll. 267–68)

– because he has *not* lost a pearl at all. Contrary to what he had imagined, he never possessed one; all he has lost in reality is a corruptible rose. The maiden then declares that only since her death has she been proved to be a pearl (capable of participating in the *summum bonum*); she is preserved in the treasure-chest of the Prince, who has always been her rightful owner as he is the only rightful possessor of all pearls. This fact about the Prince's ownership was adumbrated in the lapidary formula of the poem's very first line.[57]

The child is presented, then, under two aspects: her mortal nature (symbolized by the rose) and her immortal part (symbolized by the pearl). Her earthly father was allowed the privilege of fostering the rose for a while, but he could never possess her in so far as she is a pearl, because no man can own another's soul – not even that of the offspring of his own loins. The child is no Eurydice, one of the 'lowe thinges of the erthe', for she has an immortal soul. Moreover, it is not at all reprehensible for her earthly father to be concerned about her welfare; indeed, part of the consolation consists in the maiden's assurance that she has survived death and enjoys supreme happiness. What is wrong with the mourner's attachment to the child is revealed in an ironical passage in the debate when this man, who claims to care so much for her, complains that she enjoys too much happiness – he thinks the rank of queen is too good for her! Possessiveness leads to envy.

But in lamenting that he has lost his pearl, the narrator also commits another error: he believes that in experiencing love for the infant while she lived on Earth he had indeed attained to the possession of the *summum bonum*. He thought he possessed the unique pearl: 'I sette hyr sengeley in synglere' (l. 8). He also thought that in his affection for her he had found a happiness that was supreme – or what amounts to the same thing, he thought that she 'watȝ grounde of alle my blysse' (l. 372). It is never suggested in the poem that he was wrong in wishing to possess the unique pearl, only that he had deceived himself in supposing that he had already obtained it. In the central stanza of the poem's argument the maiden informs him that there is a pearl of great price that he can obtain; namely, the pearl which the 'jeueler' sought and for the sake of which he was prepared to sell everything he possessed. This pearl is the true *summum bonum* that is enjoyed by everyone who enters the Kingdom of Heaven. So she urges him to

> ' "... forsake þe worlde wode
> And porchace þy perle maskelles." '
>
> (ll. 743–44)

Something of the subtle pattern of relationships between the various objects and concepts to which the image of the pearl is applied should now be discernible. But there is one of its major applications that I have not yet discussed: I mean the petition in the final lines that we may all be 'precious perleȝ vnto his [the Prince's] pay'. This statement is not just an ornamental, periphrastic way of saying: 'May we all become inhabitants of the heavenly kingdom.' It has a profounder significance that involves an element of almost mystical thought. The Kingdom of Heaven or *summum bonum* cannot be obtained, in the way that a material object can, by exercising the acquisitive impulse. If he would purchase it, a man must undergo a subjective transformation into something that may be prized by God; *cupiditas* must give place to *caritas*. In order to obtain the pearl it is, paradoxically, necessary to become one. The author may be alluding to the text: 'The Kingdom of God is within you.'[58] At the same time the notion of becoming pearls ourselves alludes to the restoration of the Divine image in man; the Lamb is Himself referred to by the maiden as 'my dere juelle' (l. 795). It is in this sense that everyone may possess the pearl of great price, although it is unique.

But how is this inward transformation to be brought about? Presumably, the only way to become a pearl is to follow, as far as possible, the example of the only major character in the poem who has proved to be one: I have already remarked that one of the commonplaces of the *consolatio mortis* was to exhort the bereaved to imitate the virtues of the deceased.[59] In discussing the figure of the child I have indicated in what sense the mourner can do this: he must imitate what she typifies 'figurally'[60]; he must be reborn into a state of humility and innocence, for these are the qualities that will make him pleasing to the Prince. The fact that the only way to obtain the pearl is by becoming as a little child is also suggested structurally by the poet's juxtaposing, at the centre of his composition, the two Gospel texts about the way to enter the Kingdom of Heaven; the one concerning the figure of the child, the other the image of the pearl.[61]

The narrator would hardly have been moved to imitate the virtues of the infant and so become a pearl pleasing to the Prince, if she had not monopolized his affections while she lived in this world. His sense of total loss after the death of the beloved child left in him an emptiness so great that it could be satisfied only by the possession of the Sovereign Good itself. At the same time his meditations upon the precious qualities that she typified led him to an understanding of the surest means by which to arrive at the supreme happiness. It should now be clear why I cannot agree with Conley's assertion that 'the lost pearl' was only a transient and imperfect good. Certainly the narrator's possessive attitude towards the child was improper and he was mistaken in supposing that he had already acquired the ultimate and sovereign happiness in the delight he derived from his affection for her while she lived on Earth. But his complete surrender of his heart to love for the infant prefigured the price that must be paid to purchase the unique heavenly pearl, just as the child herself is a 'type' of what he must become spiritually in order to enjoy the sovereign happiness.

When examining the poet's use of the 'topic' of the *opportunitas mortis* I also suggested that he came to believe that Divine

Providence sent the child to him and withdrew her prematurely in order to draw his heart after her to a desire for the pearl of great price; although he was unaware of this at the time of her death.[62] In a brief poem, based upon the same Gospel text as our poem, and entitled 'The Pearl', George Herbert describes how Divine Grace guided him through the labyrinth of worldly vanities and distractions to the only proper object for his love. He employs a memorable image:

> 'Yet through these labyrinths, not my grovelling wit,
> But thy silk twist let down from heav'n to me,
> Did both conduct and teach me, how by it,
>   To climbe to thee.'[63]

The wit of the mourner in *Pearl* is no less abject and grovelling, but his road is less labyrinthine: from the moment of the child's birth he had been both conducted and taught how to climb to the sovereign good by means of a string of pearls let down to him from heaven.

This conclusion makes it necessary to look again at the use of the image of the pearl in the opening stanzas. In an earlier section of the present chapter I placed this usage within the category of *aenigma*: the author conceals the literal narrative of the child's death under the guise of a lament for a lost pearl. However, it must now be admitted that this episode can be regarded as an example of enigma only when considered locally, in isolation from the rest of the poem. In the total context of the poem it appears that in these opening stanzas the poet is concealing the 'historical' fact in order ultimately to reveal a profounder truth. Historical experience is regarded as valuable only in so far as it is related to eternal truth; the child's death is ultimately seen as a significant experience for the mourner, mainly in so far as it opens his eyes to the true and eternal source of his longing. It is therefore fitting that this historical event should be described in terms of pearl imagery – in terms of the currency of the Kingdom of Heaven – even though this has the effect of temporarily obscuring the 'historical' sense of the opening stanzas at a first reading of the poem. What seems at first to be a piece of mere mystification proves to be part of the representation of a genuine mystery.

PART THREE

SOURCES
FOR THE CHARACTERIZATION
OF THE MAIDEN

Introductory

In order to represent the apparition of the child's beatified soul, the author has to supply her with a visionary body of appropriate stature and appearance; with suitable clothing; and with arguments that will justify her status in the Kingdom of Heaven and that will console her earthly father.

Scholars have provided explanations of several details of the poet's presentation of her. There is, for example, the fact that, although she died before she was two years old, she appears to the dreamer as a maiden of adult stature. Osgood has observed that this is in accordance with St. Augustine's teaching about the body which those who die in infancy will assume after the General Resurrection.[1] It is true that Osgood seems to have forgotten that the maiden's body has not yet risen from the dead: at l. 857 she says, referring to herself and the other brides of the Lamb: 'Alþaȝ oure courseȝ in clotteȝ clynge'. But, as it is necessary for her to assume a 'visionary body' in order to manifest herself to the dreamer, it is appropriate that this body should have the appearance of the one which, according to the highest patristic authority, she will assume after the General Resurrection. Together with her adult stature goes the ability to communicate with the dreamer in adult language and concepts. Another observation made by Osgood is that her costume is cut according to the fashions of the later fourteenth century[2]; she is also appropriately adorned with pearls, and her robes are white because she is included in the procession of the hundred and forty-four thousand virgin brides of the Lamb. She wears the white 'coroun', or aureole, of virginity. There has been disagreement among scholars about the status that the poet accords her in the heavenly kingdom. René Wellek, however, was able to show that the author's opinion on this matter was not heterodox.[3] In order to demonstrate this he cites Papal decrees and more or less contemporary theological controversies.

The fundamental reason for the poet's presenting the maiden in the way that he does is that she had died while in a state of post-baptismal innocence. This simple fact, I believe, affords the true explanation of the way in which she is dressed as well as the essential reason for the status that she possesses in heaven. I shall suggest later that the best commentary on the author's intentions is to be found, not in theological disputations, Papal decrees or Biblical commentaries, but in liturgical contexts – both in the text of the liturgy itself and in the principal commentaries on it that were compiled during the twelfth and thirteenth centuries. Besides providing sources for the details I have just mentioned, these texts and commentaries supply practically all the arguments that the maiden uses in the course of her *apologia*. It is a reasonable assumption that, if the poet could have encountered these supposedly controversial doctrines in such an uncontroversial source as the text of the liturgy and the standard commentaries upon it, he would probably have taken them for granted. So there is no need to assume that he was familiar with the niceties of contemporary theological controversies on the subject of the salvation of those who die in infancy.

These elements in the characterization of the maiden, which the author could have derived from liturgical sources, are blended with others that belong to the poetic traditions of the later Middle Ages; mainly literary procedures and formulas of imagery and diction, some of which are set forth in the twelfth-century *Artes Poeticae*, but all of which are commonplace in the Latin and vernacular poetry of the succeeding centuries. He also derives details of characterization from the realm of *courtoisie* and other secular sources. His blending of the various elements is sometimes quite subtle, but its very success has perhaps been partly responsible for disguising from the modern reader the poem's true *sentence*.

Throughout the following chapters all references to the text of the liturgy (i.e. to the *Missal, Breviary, Processional,* etc.) follow the use of Sarum, unless otherwise stated.[4] Although other medieval English rites existed, the Use of Sarum was the English rite *par excellence* in the fourteenth century; it was, for example, the one used at Oxford. The liturgical commentary to which I most often refer is the *Rationale Divinorum Officiorum* by Durandus of Mende.[5] This work is to liturgical writings what the *Summa Theologiae* of St. Thomas Aquinas is to theological compilations. It makes use of all previous writings on this subject that are of any importance, and marks the culminating point in the history of this species of commentary. After the composition of the *Rationale* towards the end of the thirteenth century, no work of comparable importance appeared.[6] There are, however, two earlier sources (both of the twelfth century) that will be mentioned in this argument, although they were both used by Durandus. The first of these consists of the writings of Honorius (usually known as 'Honorius of Autun'), in particular his *Gemma Animae, Sacramentarium,* and sermons in the collection *Speculum Ecclesiae.*[7] There is a certain amount of material among these writings which is of particular interest for the present argument, but which is not included by Durandus in his *Rationale.* The other source is the work of Johannes Belethus, rector of the University of Paris, which has the same title as that of Durandus.[8] Although this work has little of relevance that is not also mentioned by Durandus, occasional references to it are given below, because there is some definite evidence of its being known in England: it was used by Bartholomaeus Anglicus (Bartholomaeus de Glanvilla) in the portion of his encyclopaedia, *De Proprietatibus Rerum,* that is entitled 'Of Times' (Book 9) in Trevisa's translation. He acknowledges his indebtedness to Belethus in Book IX, chapter 28: 'All this is take & drawe of the sentence of John Beleth, whose auctorite is solemne in holy chirch namely in ordening of office & service of holi chirch.'[9]

CHAPTER SEVEN

The Maiden as an Innocent

(i) THE LITURGY FOR CHILDERMAS

Miss Elizabeth Hart has shown how a knowledge of the liturgy for Holy Innocents' Day will elucidate a certain difficulty in *Pearl*.[1] She observes that the poet's inclusion of an infant in the procession of the hundred and forty-four thousand virgins of *Revelation* xiv may be explained by the fact that this passage occurs in the Missal as the Epistle for Innocents' Day. She also notices how Chaucer, in the *Prioress's Tale*, included his child martyr in this procession[2] and a few stanzas later called his mother 'This newe Rachel',[3] alluding to the closing words of the Gospel for the same day: 'Vox in Rama audita est, ploratus et ululatus multus: Rachel plorans filios suos, et noluit consolari, quia non sunt' (*Matt.* ii). In *Pearl* there is, of course, no question of martyrdom, but Miss Hart does not fail to notice that the Gospel for the day mentions the age of the Innocents at the time of their death as 'a bimatu et infra' (*Matt.* ii, 16), and that the dreamer remarks to the child: 'Þou lyfed not two ȝer in oure þede'. Miss Hart remarks that 'the association of the Innocents with this procession must have been common throughout the Middle Ages, being brought home to the laity by means of homilies and sermons'.

The present chapter is concerned to support this view by suggesting that the association would have been brought home by even more striking means than homilies and sermons alone, and by attempting to show that the homilies, sermons, and other liturgical pieces prescribed for this particular Feast, will account for other interesting and important details in *Pearl*.

(ii) THE PROCESSION OF THE INNOCENTS; THE BOY
BISHOP; THE LITURGICAL DRAMA

One way in which the association of the Innocents with the

faultless company who follow the Lamb would have been brought home in the fourteenth century is through the offices of the Breviary, in which various portions of the Epistle for the Mass appear as Antiphons and Responses. At Vespers on St. John's Day (the Vigil of the Feast in question) a *responsorium* beginning with the words 'Centum quadraginta . . .' is chanted; this versicle and other portions of the Epistle recur in every office for the day itself and upon its octave. There is no need to suppose that the poet would have to be a religious in order to become familiar with the Breviary, or that he was less acquainted with his 'Antiphoner' than the schoolchildren in *The Prioress's Tale*.[4] Thus, a detail in the Epistle that left only a slight impression would be confirmed by the antiphons, if only for the reason that when a few words are sung or chanted they are – *pace* Wyclif – apt to call more attention to themselves than when they occur in the middle of a long passage that is read or intoned at a comparatively faster speed. His familiarity with the Breviary could also account for our author's remembering, and expecting his audience to remember, the mere detail in the Gospel narrative about the precise age of the Innocents, since the antiphon between the first and second psalms for Lauds on Innocents' Day consists of the words: 'A bimatu et infra occidit multos pueros Herodes propter Dominum.'[5] It also occurs as the first antiphon for Terce.

The effect made by the text of the Breviary would, in the fourteenth century, have been enhanced by certain ceremonies and customs which were observed on that occasion, particularly by those associated with the institution of the Boy Bishop.[6] In the Middle Ages the feast of the Holy Innocents was recognized as the special property of children, just as St. Stephen's Day was claimed by the deacons as their own.[7] Children played a prominent part in the offices for the Feast, beginning with Vespers on St. John's Day, where the Sarum Breviary gives the following rubric:

> '*Tunc eat processio puerorum ad altare Innocentium, vel Sanctae Trinitatis, cum capis sericis et cereis illuminatis in manibus suis, cantando, R.* Centum Quadraginta . . . etc.'[8]

Anyone who witnessed this procession could not fail to perceive the association of the Innocents and the company described in

H

Revelation xiv. But what is still more important for my present purpose is the fact that anyone who witnessed this procession (and similar processions on the following day) would be inclined to associate the antiphon 'Centum Quadraginta' and the company of which it sings with children in general.

The celebration of the figure of the child, and of the state of Innocence which it represents, culminated in the practice of electing the Boy Bishop, who normally took office at Vespers on St. John's Day when, during the singing of the *Magnificat*, the precentor surrendered his staff of office at the reference to the deposition of the mighty from their seat. A child was invested with the authority (within prescribed limits) of a bishop, and even went so far as to preach a sermon. Unfortunately, no text of any such sermon preached before the late fifteenth century is extant, but a reference to the practice is to be found in a will of 1328.[9] Of the three late examples that have been preserved, one (preached in Gloucester Cathedral) takes for its text – as might be expected – *Matthew* xviii, 3; it dwells upon the Christian new birth and urges the audience themselves to become as little children.[10] Vestments of considerable expense were provided for the boy: an inventory of St. Paul's, London, of 1295 mentions a white mitre embroidered with flowers; another refers to a new white mitre with orphreys, used on these occasions.[11] One of the symbolic functions of the Boy Bishop is indicated in another Sarum rubric concerned with the singing of the *responsorium* 'Centum Quadraginta' at Vespers on St. John's Day:

> '*Solus Episcopus Innocencium, si assit, Christum puerum, uerum et aeternum Pontificem designans incipiat,* R. Centum quadraginta . . . etc.'[12]

From this account it can be seen that the feast of the Holy Innocents was made the occasion for the exaltation of the ideas of humility and innocence embodied in the figure of the child, who is, for the occasion, set in authority over his elders to admonish them and to be imitated by them. So, if he was acquainted with these practices, our author would have a clear precedent for putting a discourse on humility, innocence and spiritual renewal into the mouth of the dreamer's former child, as well as for placing her in the company which is described in

Revelation xiv. Further, it is reasonable to suppose that the impression made by a child, dressed in a bishop's robes with a white mitre set with flowers or gems, would not be forgotten by him or his audience. So it is possible that some part of the characterization of the transfigured child in *Pearl*, as she appears in 'a pyȝt coroune ... Hiȝe pynakled of cler quyt perle ... Wyth flurted flowreȝ perfet vpon',[13] to admonish him, with 'semblaunt sade for doc oþer erle',[14] may have been suggested by these ceremonies.[15]

There remains to be considered one other development from the liturgy for Innocents' Day that associates the victims of Herod with the hundred and forty-four thousand; namely, the liturgical drama of the slaughter of the Innocents. Unfortunately, texts of the liturgical dramas performed in England have not survived, but E. K. Chambers believes that there is evidence that they continued to be performed side by side with the vernacular Mysteries in the fourteenth century.[16] Karl Young has shown that the texts of the dramas that have survived all belong to a French development.[17] In a version in a service book from Laon Cathedral the choir boys enter in procession, supporting a lamb and singing: 'Ecce Agnus Dei, ecce qui tollit peccata mundi.'[18] More interesting is the example in the Fleury play-book (from a thirteenth-century MS. at Orleans).[19] It begins with the following rubric:

> '*Ad interfectionem puerorum, inducantur* Innocentes *stolis albis, et gaudentes* [gradientes?] *per monasterium, orent Dominum dicentes* "Quam gloriosum etc.". *Tunc Agnus ex improviso veniens, portans crucem, antecedat eos huc et illuc, et illi sequentes cantent:* "Quam gloriosum est regnum./Emitte Agnum, Domine" (*Isa.* xvi, 1).'

Another direction reads:

> '*Interea* Innocentes *adhuc gradientes post Agnum decantent:*
> Agno sacrato pro nobis mortificato,
> Splendorem patris, splendorem virginitatis,
> Offerimus Christo sub signo numinis [*MS.* luminis] isto ...'

– the (somewhat corrupt) text continues with a reference to Herod. Thus, the Epistle is dramatized as well as the incident that is narrated in the Gospel.

Anyone who believes that *Pearl* is more a *consolatio* than an elegy will be particularly interested by another episode in the drama. The reference at the conclusion of the Gospel to Rachel's lamentation and her refusal to be consoled is represented. She appears with two 'consolatrices', who ask her why she weeps for those who possess the Kingdom of Heaven; but she persists in her grief. Eventually an angel appears above the prostrate forms of the slaughtered children, saying: 'Sinite paruulos et nolite eos prohibere ad me venire; talium est enim regnum caelorum' (*Matthew* xix, 14). At these words, the children rise and enter the choir. The various aspects of the liturgy for the day are amalgamated into this piece, which brings out the association of the children with the Lamb and with the Apocalyptic procession. It is impossible to say whether any representation of this kind was known in England in the fourteenth century, but the example is instructive, in any case, because it illustrates the way in which the liturgy for the day was interpreted, and indicates the kind of ideas and associations that the feast evoked in the Middle Ages.[20]

In the light of what has been considered in the foregoing paragraphs, it is reasonable to suggest that a fourteenth-century poet, who was concerned with the death of an infant and her fortunes after death, would quite naturally recall the liturgy and customs of this feast when composing his *consolatio*. This hypothesis is investigated more closely in the following section.

(iii) *Lectiones* AND HOMILIES

I have mentioned that Miss Hart is aware of a possible objection to her thesis about the child in *Pearl*[21]: unlike the Innocents and the boy in *The Prioress's Tale*, this child did not suffer a martyr's death. Such an objection is, however, easily answered. The most important reason for the maiden's right to salvation is that she died soon after baptism. Similarly, the Holy Innocents died immediately after their baptism – or rather, simultaneously with it, because their martyrdom constituted their baptism, according to contemporary doctrine.[22] Thus, in establishing a relationship between the Innocents and the child in *Pearl*, the proximity of their baptism to their death is of considerable importance; the difference between the two instances is simply that, whereas the former suffered 'fullyng in blode-schedynge', the latter received 'fullyng of fonte', so that the former received martyrs' crowns in Heaven, whereas Pearl does not. The resemblances between the two instances certainly outweigh the single difference, whose significance is still further reduced when another fact is recognized: the child's baptism 'in fonte' is made efficacious only by means of a 'blode-schedynge' – although a vicarious one. Our author shows, in the course of his central argument about salvation by 'innocence' or 'ryȝt' (which, as will appear below, has other affinities with the liturgy for this day), that he is fully aware of this. In ll. 649 ff. he refers to the wound, that Christ received from the spear, as a well or font; and of the water that flowed from it he says:

> ' "Þe water is baptem, þe soþe to telle,
> Þat folȝed þe glayue so grymly grounde . . ." '
>
> (ll. 653–54)

These lines are spoken by the maiden herself as she explains the origin of her own innocence through baptism. The part that the Crucifixion plays in this process is emphasized in the middle stanza of the three that carry this explanation.[23]

With the single exception of this detail, the Innocents are represented in the liturgy as dying in the same state as Pearl. The fact that the Innocents were within two years of age at the time of their death is also emphasized in a homily in Mirk's *Festial*. He sees in this fact a special significance:

> 'Þis Innocentes þat holy chyrche syngeþ of, lyueden her wyþout schame, for þay wer all wiþin two ȝer of age . . . þes chyldyr lyued not so long forto know þe good from þe euell, but wern jslayne wiþin degre of jnnocentes. Wherfor þay lyuedon here wyþout schame.'[24]

The homily proceeds to explain the merits of Innocence. In this quotation the Innocents' early death is considered to have been a positive advantage to them, and this corresponds to what the author of *Pearl* maintains. A whole series of homilies that pursue this development of thought is afforded by the *lectiones* for Matins in the Sarum Breviary.[25] The second *lectio* is taken from Severianus, and it argues that Christ did not desert these children in permitting their early death, but was, on the contrary, bestowing a particular privilege upon them:

> 'Christus non despexit suos milites sed provexit; quibus ante dedit triumphare quam vivere; quos fecit capere sine concertatione victoriam; quos donavit coronis antequam membris; quos voluit virtutibus vitia praeterire; ante caelum possidere quam terram. Praemisit ergo Christus suos milites non anisit.'[26]

The implications of the word 'milites' in this quotation, as well as all references to martyrdom in those that follow, must be discounted for the purpose of the present argument. The point is that these passages are all concerned with children who suffer death before they are two years old.

The third *lectio* broaches the subject of salvation by Grace or merit and comes to the conclusion that is presupposed by our author; namely, that infants, who have not the power to earn their glory through meritorious deeds, are saved through Grace, since, for adult and infant alike, eternal life is a divine gift and is not due to human deserts. This homily, like the previous one, is concerned with martyrdom, but allowance can easily be made for that.

> 'Hoc loco attendat auditor, et intelligat martyrium non constare per meritum, sed venire per gratiam. In parvulis, quae voluntas, quod arbitrium, ubi captiva fuit et ipsa natura? De martyrio ergo demus totum Deo, nichil nobis. Vincere dyabolum, corpus tradere, contemnere viscera, tormenta expendere, lassare tortorem, capere de injuriis gloriam, de morte vitam, non virtutis humanae, sed muneris est divini.'[27]

The second series of *lectiones* ('In Secundo Nocturno') are taken from St. John Chrysostom. Before we examine the homilies themselves, it is worth considering the liturgical text with which the first one is associated. The office ('In Secundo Nocturno') begins with the antiphon: 'Norunt infantes laudare Deum, qui loqui non noverant: fiunt periti laude qui fuerant imperiti sermone.' This antiphon is followed by Psalm xiv (Vulgate),[28] 'Domine, quis habitabit?', after which comes another antiphon on the same Psalm: 'Exigitur itaque infantium aetas in laudem, quae delictorum non noverat crimen.' This Psalm is used in *Pearl* at ll. 678 ff., in conjunction with the similar vv. 3 and 4 of Psalm xxiv (*A.V.*; xxiii in Vulgate), dur-

ing the argument in which the maiden weighs her own claims
(as an infant) against those of the workers in the vineyard who
'stod þe long day stable', and who rely upon the length of their
service for their reward. Speaking of one of these, she says:

> ' "Where wysteȝ þou euer any bourne abate
> Euer so holy in hys *prayere*
> Þat he ne forfeted by sumkyn gate
> Þe mede sumtyme of heueneȝ clere?
> And ay þe ofter þe alder þay were,
> Þay laften ryȝt and wroȝten woghe." '
> (ll. 617–22 – my italics)

She is referring to the dreamer's earlier argument in which he
upheld the claims of the man

> ' "Þat hade endured in worlde stronge,
> And lyued in penaunce hys lyueȝ longe
> Wyþ bodyly bale hym blysse to byye . . ." '
> (ll. 476–79)

He had argued that it seemed unfair that she should have been
rewarded before such a man, and he proceeded to make a
comparison of these qualifications with her own – a comparison
which was not to her advantage:

> ' "Þou lyfed not two ȝer in oure þede;
> Þou cowþeȝ neuer God nauþer plese ne pray,
> Ne neuer nawþer Pater ne Crede." '   (ll. 483–85)

The occurrence of the word 'pray' in l. 484 and that of the word
'prayere' in l. 618 are significant. The point of the maiden's
answer to the dreamer's objection is that, although she was
ignorant of the very rudiments ('Pater' and 'Crede') of religious
instruction, she could nevertheless 'plese' God, even if she could
not 'pray' to Him. The reason for this is – she asserts – that she
is undefiled by any fleck of sin, because she has never known
any. In fact, she answers to the description, of the man fit to
stand in God's holy place, that is delineated in Psalm xxiv, 4
(*A.V.*). This is precisely the point which the antiphons 'In
Secundo Nocturno' make about the Innocents who died before
they were two years old. In the *lectio* (iv) that follows, St. John
Chrysostom elaborates this doctrine:

'Fiunt interea pueri sine magistro diserti, docti sine doctore, periti sine eruditore. Agnoscunt infantes Christum, praedicant Dominum, non quem persuasio humana docuerat, sed quem divinitas innocentibus inspirabat. Cessant enim humana cum divina tractantur: quia humana ipsa prodesse non poterunt, nisi divinorum solatio subleventur. Necesse est enim terrena succumbere, cum caelestia praedicantur; naturalia silere, cum virtutes loquuntur. Exigitur itaque infantium aetas in laudem, quae delictorum non noverat crimen.'[29]

The liturgy for Childermas goes some way towards accounting for the presence of certain details in the poet's characterization of the maiden, as well as providing a possible source for some of the doctrines about the salvation of those who die in infancy, which are asserted in the *debate* between the maiden and the dreamer.[30] There remain some important details and arguments of which it gives no account. But there are other liturgical writings that supply what is here missing and confirm much of what has already been conjectured.

CHAPTER EIGHT

The Privileges of the Newly Baptized

(i) THE DESCRIPTION OF THE MAIDEN

The maiden is the subject of something like a formal *effictio* that occurs between ll. 161 and 240. Several of the details of her appearance that are stated there and elsewhere in the poem conform to the paradigm of ideal feminine beauty that is often associated with formal descriptions of ladies in medieval literature: for example, she has golden hair and 'yȝen graye', and her complexion is compared to the 'flour-de-lys'. The whiteness of her complexion is emphasized by two other stereotyped similes: 'Hyr vysage whyt as playn yuore' and 'Her ble more blaȝt þan whalleȝ bon'. But one detail of the regular paradigm is absent: it was customary to mention the blend of white and red in the lady's cheeks and to express this idea by means of a simile about lilies mingling with red roses. In the account of the maiden's 'colour' there is no mention of red roses. The reason for this departure from the usual pattern is, of course, that the poet wishes the maiden to look as much as possible like a pearl. This fact is clearly brought out in ll. 215–16, where her 'depe colour' is compared to that of the pearls that are set in the embroidery of her dress. In fact, the poet is here observing a precept laid down by one of those very rhetoricians whose *Artes Poeticae* raised the description to the place of honour among methods of *amplificatio* and helped to establish the almost invariable features of the paragon of female beauty. Matthew of Vendôme stipulates: 'Debet autem qualibet persona ab illo intitulari epitheto quod in ea prae coeteris dominatur.'[1] 'White' is the epithet that predominates in the initial description of the maiden, and the final impression of her appearance that we carry away from the poem is of her whiteness: the very last visual impression of the heavenly country that the dreamer receives before his expulsion is of 'my lyttel quene . . . þat watȝ so *quyt*' (ll. 1147–50).

Just as the description of the maiden's personal appearance is affected by the poet's desire to make her look like a pearl, so the way in which she is dressed is determined by considerations of symbolic propriety. If we discount the fashionable cut of her raiment and disregard its other ornamental details, we find that her attire consists basically of two things: her white robes and her crown or mitre, 'Hiȝe pynakled of cler quyt perle'. She wears the white robes because she belongs to the company that follows the Lamb. But we saw in the last chapter that it is necessary to ask why she is entitled to join that company. The crown has been identified by editors as the 'aureole' that a virgin is entitled to wear in Heaven. Indeed, the maiden herself says that the Lamb 'coronde [me] clene in vergynté' (l. 767). But much earlier in the poem she had stated that He 'Corounde me *quene* in blysse to brede' (l. 415). That is surely the primary significance of her crown: the debate about her status as queen occupies a far more important place in the scheme of the poem than does the later exchange about her status as a virgin bride of the Lamb. In the next section I shall show that the basis of the maiden's apparel consists of nothing other than the ceremonial dress of the newly baptized. These vestments carried certain symbolic significations that are of considerable relevance to the meaning of *Pearl*.

(ii) THE SIGNIFICANCE OF THE MAIDEN'S 'LIVERY'
Honorius 'of Autun', in the course of a commentary on the baptismal rites celebrated on Holy Saturday, remarks that when the neophyte emerges from the font:

> 'Deinde mitra capiti ejus imponitur, veste alba induitur, quia in regnum et in sacerdotium assumitur. Per mitram corona regni, per albam sacerdotalis dignitas exprimitur, quia videlicet Christi regis et sacerdotis membrum efficitur. Per albam quoque vestem innocentia designatur, quia hanc nunc per Christum in baptismo recipit, quam in primo parente amisit.' (*Gemma Animae*, III, cxi)[2]

The final chapter of the first book of the same work (cap. cxliii) is entitled 'Baptizati albas portant vestes', and reads as follows:

'Baptizati autem ideo vestes albas portant, quae amissam innocentiam se recepisse insinuant. Illorum *mitra* regni coronam, *alba* vero sacerdotii praefert stolam. Jam enim facti sunt reges et sacerdotes et Christi regis et sacerdotis cohaeredes.'[3]

Honorius is speaking of the baptism of adult catechumens in the days when baptism by immersion was practised. This is because he is not so much concerned to explain the sacrament of baptism itself, or the contemporary baptismal rite, as to consider the liturgical ceremonies of Holy Saturday, for an understanding of which a knowledge of the baptismal practices of the primitive Church is necessary.[4] Thus, although the ceremonies that he describes had become generally outmoded by the time at which he was writing, and had been replaced by something much nearer to the modern Roman baptismal rite,[5] the memory of them was nevertheless kept alive by the liturgy for Holy Saturday and Easter Week. What I would emphasize here is the fact that since the author of *Pearl* represents the child in Heaven as having acquired full adult stature in body and in intellect, it is fitting that the basis of her 'livery' should be the dress of the adult catechumen rather than the simplified adaptation of it that was placed upon infants at their baptism during the Middle Ages.

The question of the relationship between the dress of the catechumen and that of baptized infants must now be considered. In the baptism of infants, the counterpart to the white robes of the catechumens was certainly the cloth of white linen known as the *chrisom*, and, since it was placed on the infant's head, it would do duty for the *corona* or *mitra* as well. The way in which this adaptation of the catechumen's dress was brought about can be seen from the following remark by Johannes Belethus, which occurs in his commentary on the liturgy for Holy Saturday:

'Inuncto chrismate baptizato, imponitur capite ejus chrismale, rotunda quaedam mitra quae coronam vitae significat, vel candida induitur vestis, quae ad similitudinem cuculli ex albissimo panno conficitur filo rubro supertexto. Candida illa vestis innocentiae stolam designat, quae nobis redditur in baptismo . . .'[6]

The detail of the red thread seems to have been only a local addition and need not concern us.[7] This passage should make it clear how the *chrisom* is related to both the *corona* and the *alba*. The observations of Durandus on the significance of the dress of the newly baptized are still more explicit. He remarks that in certain places the white robe is given to the neophyte in token of priesthood, and 'quaedam rotunda mitra, signum coronae regni vitae, quia ipse est membrum Christi, qui est rex et sacerdos'.[8] He shows that there is Scriptural authority for this doctrine in I *Peter* ii, 9:

> 'Omnes enim veri christiani reges, et sacerdotes dicuntur, unde Petrus Apostolus ait: "Vos autem genus electum, regale sacerdotium". Reges, quia seipsos et alios regunt . . . etc.'.[9]

The second verse of this chapter of St. Peter's epistle shows that the apostle was himself thinking of those who have been reborn into the Christian community.[10] So these liturgical commentators all agree that baptism carries with it the privilege of kingship in Christ's kingdom. If, therefore, a child were to die soon after baptism, so that it was still within what Mirk calls 'degre of jnnocentes' at the time of its death, it would acquire the status of king (or queen) upon entering the Kingdom of Heaven.

This very point is the central subject of the first part of the *debate* in *Pearl*; it has also been the subject of controversy among students of the poem. This controversy has ranged in two directions. First, it has been suggested that in the fourteenth century it would have been heretical to believe that a baptized infant could be saved; and, second, that it was heretical of the poet to argue that in Heaven everyone is 'payed inlyche/ wheþer lyttel oþer much be hys rewarde'.[11] Professor Wellek disposed of both these charges by referring to theological controversies of the time, and it is not intended to renew this dispute here.[12] What is here suggested is that there is no need to suppose that the poet had an expert knowledge of the theological controversies of the time; the essence of his argument can be found in these twelfth- and thirteenth-century commentaries on the liturgy.

Doctrines that closely resemble those formulated by the

commentators in the course of their discussion of the dress of the newly baptized are present in the poem. The 'rotunda mitra' is, according to our commentators, a symbol of the *corona* of the Kingdom of Heaven. The maiden in *Pearl* is, of course, not represented as wearing a baptismal head-dress, but this heavenly crown which it symbolizes. She declares that the Lamb 'Corounde me quene in blysse to brede . . .', although she was of a tender age when she died. The dreamer, aware of the fact that in any given kingdom there can be only one king and one queen, asks her whether she is the Queen of Heaven. The maiden explains that the Kingdom of Heaven has a mysterious 'property' (l. 446), whereby everyone who becomes an inhabitant also becomes a king or queen. The dreamer objects that he could understand her being a countess or 'lady of lasse aray' because she died before she was two years of age without knowing 'Pater or Creed', whereas the positions of greater honour should be reserved for those who have had to endure more on Earth. But these objections are shown to be irrelevant, since 'Of more and lasse in Godeȝ ryche . . . lys no joparde' (ll. 601 ff.). At this point the maiden clinches her argument by referring to the privileged status of the newly baptized (ll. 613–72), who are in a stronger position by virtue of their innocence than those who have lived longer and had time to lose it (and so to forfeit the privileges acquired at baptism) – even if it is still possible for them to regain it. It is true that in the poem it is never explicitly stated that the neophyte becomes a king by virtue of his baptism, but this idea is clearly presupposed throughout this argument. Since the neophyte is a co-heir with Christ of God's kingdom,[13] it follows that if a child dies while still in its baptismal innocence, it will, when it goes to Heaven, be 'Sesed in alle hys herytage' (l. 417).

At ll. 457–68 the maiden refers to the doctrine of the mystical body of Christ, in order to illustrate her statement in the previous stanza about the mysterious 'property' of the Kingdom of Heaven. The fact that the poet chooses to put this doctrine into her mouth at this point in her argument provides another link with the status of the newly baptized. It will be recalled that Honorius declares that the *mitra* and the *alba* are given to the newly baptized, 'quia . . . Christi regis et sacerdotis *membrum* efficitur' – he becomes a king (our author is not concerned in the poem with the priestly status) by becoming 'a longande lym to þe Mayster of myste'.[14] The point I would emphasize is that the poet does not simply derive the doctrinal material for this stanza from I *Corinthians* xii (where, incidentally, there is a direct allusion to baptism at *v.* 13), but uses this text to illustrate and support his argument that the inhabitants of the heavenly kingdom can all be kings without depriving one another of their kingship. This is precisely what the liturgical commentators say, when they discuss the status of the newly baptized.

Having considered the liturgical elements in the poem that are centred upon the signification of the 'coroune', we may now examine those that are associated with the other basic part of the maiden's dress; namely, her white robes. In quotations that have already been made from the three principal liturgical writers who are mentioned in this study, it was stated that the white vestments of the newly baptized signify the innocence which was lost through Adam and restored through the sacrament of baptism. The poet makes no explicit statement about what is signified by the white robes, but the argument of the poem shows that the innocence which the maiden received at baptism is an important element in her characterization. It is the subject of the central portion of the debate about innocence and 'riȝt'. As soon as the subject of innocence is introduced at ll. 625 ff., it is associated with baptism, and the two succeeding stanzas discuss the institution of this sacrament through the Crucifixion as a means of restoring what was withdrawn from mankind through Adam's sin. Certainly, innocence is the maiden's principal virtue, comprehending within itself subsidiary virtues such as chastity, virginity and purity.

The maiden's white robes are mentioned for the first time at l. 197: 'Al blysnande whyt watȝ hir beau biys'. In defence of the emendation of MS. *uiys*, Gordon shows that the line is a rendering of *Revelation* xix, 8, which states that it was allowed to the bride of the Lamb to clothe herself in shining white bysse.[15] As that verse from *Revelation* is unquestionably the source of this line, it may seem an act of supererogation to inquire any further into the significance of the word *biys*. Nevertheless, it is interesting to see that Durandus associates it with baptism and with the new, supernatural life that is bestowed by the sacrament. Like Honorius and Belethus, he remarks that the alb, or white robe, is the appropriate one for those who are reborn through baptism.[16] In III, iii, 1, he says that the Alb is made of bysse, or linen, because it is written: 'for the fine linen is the righteousness of saints' (*Revelation* xix, 8). In the next paragraph he remarks that *byssus* is an Egyptian linen, whose whiteness is produced by beating – and he goes on to give an allegorical meaning for this. It is not the allegorical signification given here that is of interest to us, however, but the one which is given in §5 of the same chapter, where he observes that the alb, because it is made of linen, is completely unlike the garments made from the skins of dead animals which Adam put on after the Fall, and, therefore, it symbolizes the new supernatural life that is given in baptism, and exemplified in Christ. For the same reason, the white vestments are a fitting dress for Christ, the head of His mystical body, as well as for those who have become members (limbs) through baptism:

> 'Porro, secundum quod capiti, scilicet Christo, convenit alba, quae est lineum vestimentum, longissime distans a tunicis pelliceis, quae ex mortuis animalibus fiunt, quibus Adam vestitus est post peccatum, novitatem vitae significat, quam Christus et habuit, et docuit, et tribuit in baptismo, de qua dicit Apostolus: "[Expellentes] veterem hominem cum actibus suis ... et induite novum, qui secundum Deum creatus est" (*Eph.* iv). Nam in transfiguratione "resplenduit facies ejus sicut sol, et vestimenta ejus facta sunt alba, sicut nix" (*Matt.* xvii). Semper enim vestimenta munda fuerunt, et candida, quia "peccatum non facit, nec inventus est dolus in ore ejus" (I *Peter* ii).'[17]

So, when the neophyte puts on the white robe, he assumes, not only the virtue of innocence, but the new, supernatural life as well. Moreover, he also puts on the robes that are worn by the inhabitants of the Heavenly Kingdom and the garments that are, above all, those most fitting for Christ. In fact, he puts on Christ's own livery.

The white garments of the maiden in *Pearl* have much the same pattern of interrelated functions and meanings. It would be possible to tabulate the various significations of the white robes, both in *Pearl* and in liturgical practice, according to the fourfold allegorical system of the theologians and Biblical com-

mentators – at least, in a fairly loose, analogical manner. Their
'tropological' meaning would be 'innocence'; 'allegorically'
they would symbolize rebirth in Christ, whose own livery they
are; 'anagogically' they would represent the fact that baptism
entitles the neophyte to become after death one of the white-
robed company of the New Jerusalem. The liturgical commentators did, indeed, regularly make use of this fourfold
method of interpretation.[18] A particular instance of their doing
this will serve to introduce a final observation. The example is
not directly concerned with white robes, but it does establish
the association between the newly baptized and the hundred
and forty-four thousand faultless virgins. Honorius 'of Autun',
in the course of his commentary on the liturgy for Holy
Saturday, considers the reason for the singing of the canticle,
'Sicut cervus desiderat', during the procession to the font, which
was undertaken on that day and was repeated daily throughout
the following Easter Week. He sees an anagogical significance
in this practice:

> 'Anagoge, id est sensus ad superiores ducens, locutio est,
> quae de praeteritis, futuris, et ea quae in coelis est vita
> futura, sive mysticis sive apertis sermonibus disputat; unde
> catechumenis dicitur in Cantico: "Sicut cervus desiderat
> ad fontes aquarum". Canticum ideo cantatur, quia ipsi
> sunt futuri in baptismo de centum quadraginta quatuor
> milium coetu, qui cantant canticum novum, quod nemo
> potuerat dicere nisi illi.'[19]

Similarly, Durandus observes:

> 'Ideo autem Cantica cantantur, quia catechumeni,
> quorum est hujus diei officium, futuri sunt in proximo de
> coetu centum quadraginta quatuor millium cantantium
> canticum novum (*Rev.* xiv). Cantatur etiam propter
> futuram renovationem in veram innocentiam, quasi jam
> factum sit quod cito futurum sit . . .'[20]

The liturgy for Holy Saturday was instituted at a time when
baptism of adult catechumens by immersion was generally
practised, and when that sacrament was celebrated only twice
a year: on Holy Saturday and at Pentecost – of which the
former was, liturgically, the more important occasion. In the
fourteenth century, when the candidates for baptism were

infants rather than adults, and the sacrament was celebrated independently of these dates, the conditions that originally determined the structure of the liturgy for this season no longer obtained. There could, for example, be no procession of neophytes to the font throughout Easter Week. So certain adaptations were made. Thus, the procession was undertaken by the clergy and choir dressed in albs.[21] Again, although there may sometimes have been nobody to baptize on Holy Saturday,[22] the idea of baptism retained its pre-eminence in the liturgy on account of the ceremony of the blessing of the font. The liturgy would, normally, no longer be performed for the benefit of the neophyte, but for the edification of adults who had been baptized as infants. So these portions of the liturgy would acquire an allegorical rather than a literal significance. The baptismal ceremonies would provide an annual opportunity for an act of spiritual renewal; the figure of the neophyte would become a symbol, inciting the faithful to return to the state of innocence which they possessed after their baptism.

Similarly, the Epistle in the Mass for the Saturday in Easter Week, originally intended for the exhortation of the neophytes, would serve to impress upon Christians who had been baptized many years earlier a *sentence* similar to the one that is implied in *Pearl*. It was taken from I *Peter* ii and urged its hearers to lay aside guile and envy, and 'like new-born babes, desire the rational milk without guile, that thereby you may grow unto salvation'. The faithful were again urged to imitate the virtues of the infant in the Introit for the following day (Low Sunday): 'Quasi modo geniti infantes, alleluia: rationabile, sine dolo lac concupiscite, alleluia, alleluia, alleluia'.[23] The day came to be known as 'Quasimodo Sunday'.

I

CHAPTER NINE

The Maiden's Interpretation of the Parable of the Labourers in the Vineyard

In this final chapter I attempt to settle 'a poynt determynable'.

The author of *Pearl* introduces the parable of the labourers in the vineyard[1] into his poem[2] as an *exemplum* to give Scriptural authority to the maiden's argument about the justness of the reward that she receives in Heaven. In order to do this, he provides an interpretation of the parable that has disturbed some students of the poem; it has even been argued that its implications would have amounted to heresy in the fourteenth century.[3] Although Wellek[4] has shown that there is no real foundation for this charge, he was unable to produce any precedent for the idea that is at the centre of the poet's interpretation; namely, the identification of an infant who died before she was two years old with those labourers in the parable who entered the vineyard at the 'eleventh hour' or, as the poet phrases it himself, 'On oure byfore þe sonne go doun'.[5] This identification is made quite explicitly when the maiden declares: 'In euentyde into þe vyne I come.'[6] However, more recently D. W. Robertson Jr. has observed[7] that a similar interpretation is made in an eleventh-century commentary by Bruno of Asti on St. Matthew's Gospel. When he comes to consider those who entered the vineyard at the eleventh hour and who were the first to receive their payment, Bruno remarks:

'Undecim vera hora illa est quae in qualibet aetate funeri appropinquat et morti proxima est. Hanc enim horam non solum juvenes et senes, verum etiam pueri habeunt.'[8]

Since, in this interpretation, entry into the vineyard symbolizes baptism into the Church, Bruno is asserting, in effect, that those who die soon after baptism are the first to be rewarded in

Heaven. Children may be included within this category as well
as adults.

This interpretation certainly appears to contain the germ out
of which the one in *Pearl* developed. Yet there is a serious
objection to its being regarded as an adequate precedent for
the poet's interpretation. It is impossible to be certain that
Bruno, when he speaks of children (*pueri*), means to include
babes in arms among them. Anyone who is familiar with the
controversies concerning the orthodoxy of the poet's opinions
will realize that this objection is no mere quibble, but touches
upon a crucial theological point. Children are capable of
actively performing some 'Good Works' and of serving God
with a certain amount of prayer, but the maiden in *Pearl* died
before she could exercise her Free Will, while knowing 'nawþer
Pater ne Crede'[9] – the very rudiments of Christian worship.
Nevertheless, she was rewarded before those 'þat toke more
tom' and who 'swange and swat for long ʒore'[10] – by spending
their lives in prayer and penance.[11] Any interpretation must
make allowance for this fact before it can be accepted as a
satisfactory precedent for the one in *Pearl*. Bruno's interpretation is not altogether satisfactory because it is not sufficiently
explicit on this point.

But there is an interpretation of the parable that is quite
unambiguous. It is by one of the commentators to whose
writings I have referred several times already: Honorius 'of
Autun'. He interprets the times of day at which the various
workers entered the vineyard as the several ages of man's life.
Thus, those who entered at the first hour represent those who
began their service of God in infancy; those who entered at the
eleventh hour represent those who are converted in old age.
These death-bed converts are rewarded before those who
received baptism at an earlier period in their lives for the
following reason: 'Ultimis primitus denarius datur quia saepius
talibus priusquam pueris vita aeterna recompensatur.'[12] At
first sight, this statement may appear to contradict the poet's
interpretation, but, in effect, it implies nothing more than the
fact that most people die in old age rather than as children. It
is, however, the next stage in Honorius's interpretation that is
the important one for our present purpose, because he proceeds
to include those who die as infants in the same category as

those who are converted 'in decrepita aetate' and are represented by the labourers who entered the vineyard at the eleventh hour. Undoubtedly, the principle that lies behind Honorius's interpretation is identical with the one upon which Bruno bases his; namely, the importance of the proximity of baptism to death in determining priority of reward in Heaven. But, unlike Bruno, Honorius leaves us in no doubt about the applicability of his interpretation to the case of the maiden in *Pearl*:

> 'Dominus dicit sibi licere bona dare quibus velit, *quia infantibus qui nichil laboraverunt*, et in fine poenitentibus qui parum laboraverunt, prius quam his qui tota vita laboraverunt aeterna gaudia impendit.'[13]

Admittedly, the maiden claims that baptized infants, who entered the vineyard in the evening, *have* performed some labour (l. 634). But their 'labour' consists simply of the fact that 'þay wern þereine' (l. 633) – and that while in the vineyard they did not forfeit their right (bestowed at baptism) to receive the promised penny, because they 'wroʒt neuer wrang er þenne þay wente' (l. 631). According to the maiden's interpretation, the workers are deemed to have begun to labour by the very act of 'clocking in'. When Honorius mentions infants 'qui nichil laboraverunt', he is using the term *laborare* in a stricter sense to refer to good works such as those rudimentary acts of faith and of prayer that the maiden could not possibly have performed while on Earth. But this slight discrepancy does not affect the issue: clearly, if the infants to whom Honorius refers received priority in the matter of payment, the maiden was also entitled to do so.

The poet makes one allusion, in passing, that gives a possible clue to the way in which Honorius's interpretation may have reached him. The maiden introduces the parable with the words:

> ' "As Mathew meleʒ in your messe
> In sothfol Gospel of God Al-myʒt . . ." ' (ll. 497–98)

The only day in the calendar when the parable of the labourers in the vineyard occurs as the Gospel in the Mass is Septuagesima Sunday. Osgood believes that this fact is of no significance in the context, and he argues that the presence of the word 'messe' may be attributed to the demands of the rhyme and alliteration.[14] Indeed, he is able to cite two lines from *Patience* which suggest that the whole of *Pearl*, l. 497, would have come into the poet's head as a fixed, alliterative collocation:

'I herde on a halyday at a hyȝe masse,
How Mathew melede . . .'[15]

Moreover, there is an even closer resemblance in *Purity*, l. 51, which he appears to have overlooked: 'As Maþew meleȝ in his masse of þat man ryche . . .'. But it would be rash to proceed from this consideration alone to the conclusion that the poet's reference to the parable's liturgical context is necessarily fortuitous. The fact that he alludes to this particular secondary source, instead of giving a straightforward reference to the parable's Biblical context, may be significant; for it may be taken as an indication, not only of his immediate source for the parable itself, but also of the one from which he received the interpretation that is applied to it in *Pearl*.

The one place where he would almost certainly have heard an interpretation of this parable every year was at Mass on Septuagesima Sunday, because it was usual for homilies delivered at Mass to consist in expositions of the Epistle and Gospel for the day. It is, therefore, particularly interesting that Honorius's interpretation, which is apparently the only satisfactory precedent for the one in *Pearl* that has yet been discovered, actually occurs in his sermon for Septuagesima Sunday. This sermon expounds, not only the Epistle and Gospel, but all the liturgy for the day[16]; it appears to have been written as a model for less learned clerics who were obliged to preach on that day. I hesitate to draw any definite conclusion from these facts, as I have not yet discovered any evidence that succeeding generations of preachers did make use of this exemplar and, in so doing, give currency in the popular pulpit to this particular interpretation of the parable. But, whatever the route by which the interpretation reached the poet, it is interesting to find it occurring already in the twelfth century in a homiletic and non-controversial context.

APPENDIX

Editorial Punctuation of two Stanzas in Group XIV
(See above, p. 56, n. 13)

The punctuation by editors of the penultimate stanza in Group XIV is misleading, for it implies that ll. 827 and 828 are part of St. John's prophecy:

' "Hys generacyoun quo recen con,
Þat dyȝed for vus in Jerusalem?" '

(Gordon's punctuation)

Since the verb *dyȝed* in l. 828 is in the past tense, and since it clearly refers to the death of Christ, it can hardly be contained in a speech which alludes to that event as something that will happen in the future. If l. 828 is not part of the speech, then it is reasonable to suppose that neither is l. 827. The words 'Hys generacyoun quo recen con' are not put into the mouth of St John in any of the Gospel accounts, but they do occur in *Isaiah* liii, 8. This suggests that the two lines are the maiden's comment on the passage which not only relates it to the event that it predicts, but also refers it back to the earlier prophecy with which it 'accords'. Lines 825–26 also are not to be found in St. John's Gospel, but are in *Isaiah* liii. However, it is probable that the poet puts these into the Baptist's mouth in order to confirm the concordance, since they are only an expansion of the idea contained in l. 822. Readers who wish to seek some subtler reason for the presence of l. 827 may find some significance in the fact that, in St. Luke's account of the baptism of Christ (where, however, there is no reference to the 'lamb'), the evangelist actually proceeds to reckon the generation of Christ back to Adam (*Luke* iii, 23–38)!

A similar criticism must be made of the editors' punctuation of ll. 803–4, which implies that they are part of the prophecy of Isaiah. In both instances, the poet has to break off his account of the actual words of the prophet and to add a comment, in order that he may introduce the 'link-word', *Jerusalem*, into the last line of the stanza. This is not an example of the way in which the stanza-linking system hampers his expression. The 'link-word' is chosen deliberately in order to maintain the association of the Lamb with Jerusalem and, hence, to prepare the way for the allegorical exposition that is to follow in Group XVI. The culmination of this association of the two figures comes at l. 841, where the maiden speaks of 'Thys Jerusalem Lombe'.

Bibliographical Note

The following list of editions and studies of *Pearl* includes only those that are mentioned elsewhere in the present volume. I have not attempted to compile a complete list of published studies of the poem's structure and meaning.

EDITIONS

Gollancz, Sir Israel, *Pearl*, ed. with modern rendering, together with Boccaccio's *Olympia* (London, 1921).

Gordon, E. V., (ed.), *Pearl* (Oxford, 1953). The standard edition, including Select Bibliography of relevant works published before 1952. All quotations in the present volume from the text of *Pearl* are taken from this edition.

Osgood, C. G., (ed.), *The Pearl* (Boston, 1906). The introduction and notes contain some valuable information that is not incorporated in later edd. of the poem.

STUDIES

Barron, W. R. J., 'Luf-daungere' in *A Medieval Miscellany Presented to Eugène Vinaver* (Manchester, 1965), pp. 1–18.

Bishop, I., 'The Significance of the "Garlande Gay" in the Allegory of *Pearl*', *RES* (N.S.), viii (1957), pp. 12–21.

Blanch, R. J., 'Precious Metal and Gem Symbolism in *Pearl*', *The Lock Haven Review*, vii (1965), pp. 1–12. This article is reprinted in:

— (ed.) *Sir Gawain and Pearl: Critical Essays* (Bloomington and London, 1966). This anthology also contains articles, listed below, by Luttrell, Spearing (*MP*) and Wellek.

Brewer, D. S., 'The Gawain-Poet: A General Appreciation of the Four Poems', *Essays in Criticism*, xvii (1967), pp. 130–42.

Brown, C. F., 'The Author of *The Pearl* considered in the Light of his Theological Opinions', *PMLA*, xix (1904), pp. 115–53.

Carson, Mother Angela, 'Aspects of Elegy in the Middle English *Pearl*', *SP*, lxii (1965), pp. 17–27.

Chapman, C. O., 'Numerical Symbolism in Dante and the *Pearl*', *MLN*, liv (1939), pp. 256–59.

Conley, J., '*Pearl* and a Lost Tradition', *JEGP*, liv (1955), pp. 332–47.

Davis, N., Review of Gordon's edition, *M. AE.*, xxiii (1954), pp. 96–100.

— 'A Note on *Pearl*', *RES* (N.S.), xvii (1966), pp. 403–5; xviii, p. 294.

Everett, Dorothy, *Essays on Middle English Literature* (Oxford, 1955), pp. 85–96.

— and Hurnard, Naomi D., 'Legal Phraseology in a passage in *Pearl*', *M. AE.*, xvi (1947), pp. 9 ff.

Hart, Elizabeth, 'The Heaven of Virgins', *MLN*, xlii (1927), pp. 113–16.

Hieatt, Constance, '*Pearl* and the Dream Vision Tradition', *Studia Neophilologica*, xxxvii (1965), pp. 139–45.

Hillmann, Sister Mary Vincent, *The Pearl, A New Translation and Interpretation* (New York, 1961).

Kean, Patricia M., 'Numerical Composition in "Pearl" ', *Notes and Queries*, ccx (Feb. 1965), pp. 49–51.

— *The Pearl: An Interpretation* (London, 1967). This book was published after I had finished writing the text of the present study, but in time for me to refer in footnotes to the few places of any importance where Miss Kean's arguments corroborate my own. My views on Miss Kean's interpretation as a whole will appear in a forthcoming review in *M. AE.*

Luttrell, C. A., '*Pearl*: Symbolism in a Garden Setting', *Neophilologus*, xlix (1965), pp. 160–76. Reprinted in the anthology ed. by Blanch (see above).

Madeleva, Sister Mary, *Pearl: A Study in Spiritual Dryness* (New York, 1925).

Robertson, D. W., 'The "Heresy" of *The Pearl*', *MLN*, lxv (1950), pp. 152–55.

Schofield, W. H., 'The Nature and Fabric of *The Pearl*', *PMLA*, xix (1904), pp. 154–215.

— 'Symbolism, Allegory and Autobiography in *The Pearl*', *PMLA*, xxiv (1909), pp. 585–675.

Spearing, A. C., 'Symbolic and Dramatic Development in *Pearl*', *MP*, lx (1962), pp. 1–12. Reprinted in the anthology ed. by Blanch (see above).

— '*Patience* and the *Gawain* Poet', *Anglia*, lxxxiv (1967), pp. 305–29.

Watts, V. E., '*Pearl* as a *Consolatio*', *M. AE.*, xxxii (1963), pp. 34–36.

Wellek, R., '*Pearl*: An Interpretation of the Middle English Poem', *Studies in English by Members of the English Seminar of Charles University*, iv (Prague, 1933), pp. 5–33. Reprinted in the anthology ed. by Blanch (see above).

Wintermute, E., 'The Author of *Pearl* as a Herbalist', *MLN*, lxiv (1949), pp. 83–84.

Wrenn, C. L., 'On Re-reading Spenser's *The Shepheardes Calender*', *Essays and Studies by Members of the English Association*, xxix (1943), pp. 30–40; see esp. pp. 31–32.

Notes

INTRODUCTION

1. *RES* (N.S.), viii (February 1957), pp. 12–21.
2. Oxford, 1953. All my quotations from the poem follow the text of this edition.
3. *Ed. cit.*, pp. xi ff.
4. See above, p. 104.
5. I have not made any comparison between the theme of *Pearl* and those of the other poems in MS. Cotton Nero A x. Two articles on this subject have appeared recently: D. S. Brewer, 'The Gawain-Poet: A General Appreciation of the Four Poems', *Essays in Criticism*, xvii, 130–42; A. C. Spearing, '*Patience* and the *Gawain* Poet', *Anglia*, lxxxiv, 305–29. The latter article should be read in conjunction with the same author's 'Symbolic and Dramatic Development in *Pearl*', *MP*, lx, 1–12. This article has been reprinted in the anthology ed. by R. J. Blanch (see Bibliographical Note, above, p. 128). For a further comparison see the recently published book on *Pearl* by Miss P. M. Kean (see Bibliographical Note, above, p. 129), pp. 229–32, 237–42.
6. *Ed. cit.*, pp. xi–xix.
7. Admittedly, not all attempts to defend a personal interpretation are models of sanity, consistency and logic. One of the most recent is also one of the most extravagant: Mother Angela Carson, 'Aspects of Elegy in the Middle English *Pearl*', *SP*, lxii, 17–27. The author believes that the mourner laments the loss, not of a child, but of an adult mistress – a pagan immigrant from the East who had been converted to Christianity and had died after nearly two years' residence in England (cf. l. 483: ' "þou lyfed not two ʒer in oure þede" ').
8. *Ed. cit.*, pp. xiv ff.
9. See above, pp. 84 ff.
10. See above, pp. 80–88.
11. They have been collected by Gordon in the introduction to his edition, pp. xii–xiv.
12. See above, pp. 104-5.
13. 'A Note on *Pearl*', *RES* (N.S.), xvii, 403–5. He shows that l. 1208 consists of an epistolary formula that in Middle English texts of the fourteenth and fifteenth centuries was used almost exclusively by parents addressing their children. But see *ibid.*, xviii, 294.
14. *Ed. cit.*, p. xiii.
15. *Ibid.*

CHAPTER ONE

1. '*Pearl* and the Dream Vision Tradition', *Studia Neophilologica*, xxxvii, 139–45. See also P. M. Kean, *Pearl*, 28–30, 175.

2. The Latin text and an English translation of this eclogue are included by Sir Israel Gollancz in his 1921 ed. of *Pearl*.

3. *PMLA*, xix, 154–215.

4. The best survey of the early stages of this controversy – with some very perceptive comments – is by René Wellek: '*The Pearl*: An Interpretation of the Middle English Poem', *Studies in English*, IV, Charles University, Prague, 1933. The article is reprinted in the anthology ed. by R. J. Blanch (see Bibliographical Note, above, p. 128). Since the publication of Gordon's ed. there has been little support for a 'totally allegorical' approach to the poem: the most notable example of such an interpretation is the one that is advanced by Sister Mary Vincent Hillmann, *The Pearl, A New Translation and Interpretation* (New York, 1961).

5. *Essays on Middle English Literature* (Oxford, 1955), pp. 85–96.

6. *Ibid.*, p. 96.

7. On the history of the *genre* up to the fifth century A.D., see Charles Favez, *La Consolation Latine Chrétienne* (Paris, 1937); Sister Mary M. Beyenka, *Consolation in St. Augustine* (Washington, D.C., 1950). For a very brief discussion of 'Topics of Consolatory Oratory', see also E. R. Curtius, *European Literature and the Latin Middle Ages* (trans. W. R. Trask; London, 1953), pp. 80–82.

8. *Neophilologus*, xlv, 63–75.

9. *JEGP*, liv, 332–47.

10. See above, pp. 93 ff.

11. *M. AE.*, xxxii, 34–36.

12. Ed. by G. de Hartel, *CSEL*, xxx (Vienna, 1894), pp. 307–29.

13. In *A History of Christian Latin Poetry* (Oxford, 1927) J. E. Raby describes the poem as 'the first Christian elegy' (p. 105). In this he is following Boissier, *Fin du Paganisme*, iii, 89. But one of the MSS.' titles indicates that it is rather a consolation: 'item versus ejusdem consolatorii de Celso puero Pneumatii filio defuncto' (*CSEL*, xxx, 307). On Paulinus see also Pierre de Labriolle, *Histoire de la Littérature Latine Chrétienne* (new ed., Paris, 1947), pp. 481–94, but esp. Favez (*op. cit.*), which is the source of Mr Watts's account of fourth-century consolations.

14. *The Works of Henry Vaughan*, ed. L. C. Martin (second ed., Oxford, 1957), p. 345. The extract translates only a selection of lines from the corresponding passage in the original – see Martin's note, p. 724. Vaughan describes Paulinus's poem as a 'Panegyrick' (p. 344, l. 44): *consolationes* were, indeed, regarded as a branch of epideictic rhetoric.

15. (Washington, D.C., 1950), p. 15.

16. *Ibid.*, p 20.

17. *Ibid.*, p. 24.

18. *Ibid.*, p. 29.

19. *CSEL*, xxx, 315.

20. Beyenka, *op. cit.*, p. 59 (six examples of this metaphor); pp. 86 and 89.

21. *PL*, xxxix, 1599–1611.

22. Beyenka, *op. cit.*, pp. 88–89. For further discussion of the metaphor, see Favez, *op. cit.*, p. 159. See also above, p. 85.

23. See Favez, *op. cit.*, p. 68. The fact that this was still a recognized 'topic' in the Middle Ages is well attested by the way in which it is used as a somewhat

disingenuous 'ploy' in Andreas Capellanus, *De Arte Honeste Amandi*. In this passage immoderate grief is condemned also as an act of rebellion against the Divine Will: 'Nam ultra tempus legibus praestitutum lugere maritum est quidem legalia iura contemnere et animo rebelli divinae obsistere voluntati et contra eius facta temerario animo cogitare.' (*Andreae Capellani . . . De Amore*. Recensuit E. Trojel – Copenhagen, 1892 – p. 173.)

24. *Art. cit.*, p. 64.

25. *European Literature and the Latin Middle Ages*, p. 80.

26. The author of *Ancrene Riwle* says that to shun even human consolation is an act that can plunge an ancress into the deadly sin of *Accidie*: 'Sum he is abuten to makien so swuðe uleon monne uroure ðet heo ualleð ine deaðlich sor, þet is accidie, oþer into deop þouht, so ðet heo dotie.' (*The English Text of the Ancrene Riwle* ed. from Cotton MS. Nero A XIV by Mabel Day – *EETS* O.S. 225; London, 1952 – p. 100, ll. 32–34.)

Miss P. M. Kean (see Bibliographical Note, above, p. 129) in her book on *Pearl* (p. 234), cites passages from St. Bernard's sermon on the death of his brother which, in fact, involve the topic of the evil of immoderate grief; but she does not recognize it as such. Although Miss Kean is aware that the poet has a consolatory purpose, she never refers to *consolatio* as a literary *genre*. Similarly, although she has much to say about the use of rhetorical 'topoi' in *Pearl*, she does not notice the poet's use of consolatory commonplaces and standard *solacia*.

27. See Cross, *art. cit.*, p. 70, for exx. from Euripides to Chaucer.

28. *Op. cit.*, p. 13.

29. *Ibid.*, pp. 102–4. On p. 19 she notes the use of the same topic by St. Basil. See also Favez, *op. cit.*, pp. 69–70, who discusses the *solacium* that one error of the bereaved is to believe that they have an eternal right to those whom they love.

30. See above, pp. 83 and 95.

31. Augustine quotes a passage in which Cyprian makes this point. See Beyenka *op. cit.*, p. 69.

32. *PG*, xlvi, 161–91. Cited by Beyenka, *op. cit.*, p. 20, who also cites the use of this topic by St. Basil (p. 19). For further discussion, see Favez, *op. cit.*, pp. 67, 154–55.

33. Beyenka, *op. cit.*, p. 30.

34. Lines 591–628.

35. Lines 629–32, *CSEL*, xxx, 329. It is interesting to observe that in *Pearl*, l. 909, the dreamer addresses the maiden as follows: ' "Now, hynde, þat sympelnesse coneȝ enclose . . ." ' Cf. Gordon's speculations about the reason for the attribution to her of this virtue (*ed. cit.*, p. 76).

36. See above, pp. 60–61; 97–98.

37. *M. AE.*, xxxii, 36, n. 12.

38. Cross, *art. cit.*, p. 69.

39. All quotations from Chaucer in the present study follow the text in the edition of his complete works by F. N. Robinson (second edition, London, 1957).

40. See Robinson, *ed. cit.*, p. 682.

41. See Beyenka, *op. cit.*, p. 19.

42. *Ibid.*, p. 13.

43. For an attempt to show that it does offer Christian consolation, see B. F. Huppé

and D. W. Robertson, Jr., *Fruyt and Chaf: Studies in Chaucer's Allegories* (Princeton University Press; Oxford University Press, 1963). But it involves a process of total allegorization that is totally unconvincing.

44. This has led Wolfgang Clemen to deny the presence of consolatory 'topoi': *Chaucer's Early Poetry* (trans. C. A. M. Sym; London, 1963), pp. 45 and n. 4, 49. But see p. 54, n. 4.

45. See J. Lawlor, 'The Pattern of Consolation in *The Book of the Duchess*', *Speculum*, xxxi, 626–48. Reprinted in *Chaucer Criticism, vol. ii: Troilus and Criseyde and the Minor Poems*, ed. R. J. Schoeck and J. Taylor (Notre Dame, Indiana, 1961).

46. The attempts of B. H. Bronson ('*The Book of the Duchess* Re-opened', *PMLA*, lxvii, 863–81; reprinted in *Chaucer: Modern Essays in Criticism*, ed. E. Wagenknecht – New York, 1959 – pp. 271–94), Lawlor (*art. cit.*) and Clemen to demonstrate that consolation is achieved in the poem seem to me unconvincing. In his attempt to do this, Clemen is betrayed into making an insensitive and inaccurate observation that is quite uncharacteristic of him:

> 'Just as Halcyone was comforted by the reappearance of her husband in a dream, the knight was comforted by recalling his dead wife to mind as he told his own story.' (*op. cit.*, p. 31 – but see last paragraph of p. 35).

But was Halcyone comforted by the dream? Chaucer describes her reaction thus:

> 'With that hir eyen up she casteth
> And saw noght. "Allas!" quod she for sorwe,
> And deyede within the thridde morwe.' (ll. 212–14)

Very effective consolation!

47. See his final speech, ll. 280 to end. For Latin text and English translation, see Gollancz's 1921 ed. of *Pearl*, pp. 284–85.

48. *Ed. cit.*, pp. 172–73. The passage includes the following *solacia*: death as the common lot of mankind; the uselessness and impropriety of complaining against the divine will; a version of the *opportunitas mortis*; the prospect of future reunion in heaven.

49. Trans. by P. H. Wicksteed (London, 1903; reprinted, 1940), pp. 110–11. Commenting on this passage, Étienne Gilson remarks that 'after the death of Beatrice [he] had the idea of turning to the specialists in consolation in order to seek a remedy for his ailment' (*Dante The Philosopher* – trans. by David Moore; London, 1948 – p. 93). In a footnote he observes (*ibid.*, n. 1): 'Dante therefore read BOETHIUS, *De Consolatione Philosophiae*, and CICERO, *Laelius sive de Amicitia*.' Gilson refers the reader to the monograph by Favez.

50. Cicero's treatise on consolation, which he wrote to console himself at the death of his daughter Tullia, was very influential among early Christian, as well as pagan, authors of consolations. The work in its original form is now lost, but much of it has been preserved by Lactantius (see Beyenka, *op. cit.*, pp. 5, 17).

51. See above, pp. 59-60.

52. See above, p. 16.

CHAPTER TWO

1. *L'Esthétique Du Moyen Age* (Louvain, 1947), pp. 113 ff. A fuller discussion o.

the documentary evidence for this assertion is contained in vol. iii, *passim*, of the same author's *Études d'Esthétique Médiévale* (Bruges, 1946).

2. 'Numerical Symbolism in Dante and *Pearl*', *MLN*, liv, 256 ff. Gordon has exposed its main weaknesses, *ed. cit.*, p. 88, n. 2.

3. *European Literature and the Latin Middle Ages* (trans. cit.), pp. 501 ff. For treatment of numerical composition in a later period, see Alastair Fowler, *Spenser and the Numbers of Time* (London, 1964).

4. *Sir Gawain and the Green Knight*, ll. 623 ff. For a recent discussion of the numerological symbolism of the pentacle, see Roger Lass, ' "Man's Heaven", The Symbolism of Gawain's Shield', *Mediaeval Studies* (Toronto), xxviii, 354–60.

5. In his review of Gordon's edition, *M. AE.*, xxiii, 100.

6. *Notes and Queries*, ccx (Feb. 1965), pp. 49–51. But Miss Kean does not mention the piece of evidence adduced by Professor Davis.

7. Readers who enjoy such numerological speculations may find some significance in the fact that, according to one tradition, 72 was the number of years that the Virgin Mary lived on Earth. They may even find an association between the Virgin and the number 15, since the feast of her Assumption is celebrated on August 15th – almost certainly the 'hyȝ seysoun' (l. 39) when the narrator experienced his vision (see above, pp. 85-87). But these facts seem to me to be irrelevant to the context of Group XV, since the Virgin is not mentioned there, whereas the group is concerned entirely with the company that follows the Lamb; the number of maidens in the company is, moreover, spelt out accurately at ll. 869–70 (in Stanza 73).

8. It is interesting that the product of 5×12 was used as a generic large number: see Susie I. Tucker, 'Sixty as an Indefinite Large Number in Middle English', *RES*, xxv, 152–53; see also A. J. Bliss (ed.), *Sir Launfal* (London, 1960), p. 88 (n. on l. 240).

9. *Op. cit.*, p. 88.

10. *Le Roman de la Rose*, ed. by Ernest Langlois, *SATF* (Paris, 1924), v, 37.

11. A 'game of art': the classical term for exhibitions of virtuosity similar to those displayed in these poems by Herbert, or in his 'Trinitie Sunday'.

12. Kunz and Stevenson, *The Book of the Pearl* (London, 1908).

13. For descriptions in late medieval English wills of 'pairs of beads', see A. W. Pollard's ed. of *Chaucer's Canterbury Tales: Prologue* (London, 1903), p. 43 (note on l. 159).

14. See *RES* (N.S.), viii, 12–21 (and see above, p. 1; also, p. 84). In that article I remarked (*ibid.*, p. 20, n. 3) that I had not at that time been able to find any direct evidence for the existence of 'coronae' chandeliers of any type in England in the fourteenth century – although there is documentary evidence for their existence here up to the end of the thirteenth century, and more than documentary evidence of their continued existence on the Continent. I am, therefore, particularly grateful to Dr M. Q. Smith for kindly drawing my attention to a passage in H. E. Bishop and E. K. Prideaux, *The Building of Exeter Cathedral* (Exeter, 1922), p. 145, which refers to: Fabric Roll, 1312–13, that mentions a silver Corona in front of the choir altar; Fabric Roll, 1376–77, that mentions another 'in front of the Cross in the choir'.

15. I am indebted to Professor J. A. W. Bennett for drawing my attention to this

fact, as long ago as 1950, when I first mentioned to him my theory about the way in which 'coronae' candelabra could illuminate the meaning of l. 1186.

16. *The Poetry of Meditation*. First published in 1954 as Vol. 125 of *Yale Studies in English*. In the revised ed. (New Haven and London, 1962) these poems are discussed on pp. 96–112.

17. For a cogent reply to charges that the poem is marred by its 'artificial' verse-form, see Gordon, *ed. cit.*, pp. xxxvi ff.

18. *Op. cit.*, p. 87.

19. See Th.-M. Charland, *Artes Praedicandi; Contribution à l'Histoire de la Rhétorique au Moyen Age* (Paris and Ottawa, 1936). As his frontispiece he reproduces a MS. illustration of an 'Arbor de Arte Praedicandi'. The text (with English translation) of a brief, but comprehensive, *Ars Praedicandi* is edited by H. Caplan, 'A Late Medieval Treatise on Preaching' in *Studies in Rhetoric and Public Speaking in Honour of J. A. Winans* (New York, 1925), pp. 61–91. For further discussion of this treatise, see H. Caplan, 'Rhetorical Invention in Some Medieval Treatises on Preaching', *Speculum*, ii, 284 ff. For references to the ingenious, topiary shapes assumed in the development sections of some sermons, see W. O. Ross (ed.), *Middle English Sermons* (*EETS*, O.S., No. 209), p. xlix, n. 4; he mentions 'pyramidal', 'plane', 'cubical' and 'circular' forms assumed by the arrangements of the divisions and subdivisions of the *thema*.

For an account of how a knowledge of the *Artes Praedicandi* may help us to understand the structure of another fourteenth-century English poem, see Elizabeth Salter, *Piers Plowman: An Introduction* (Basil Blackwell, Oxford, 1962), pp. 24 ff., and especially A. C. Spearing, *Criticism and Medieval Poetry* (London, 1964), pp. 68 ff. in his chapter on 'The Art of Preaching and *Piers Plowman*'.

20. Such symmetrical devices and similar correspondences are used, however, in music – another art that unfolds itself in the temporal dimension. An apt example of musical symmetry is afforded by the 'crab' canon in the remarkable three-part rondeau 'Ma fin est mon commencement' by our poet's elder contemporary, Guillaume de Machaut. Classical 'sonata-form' also depends upon partial symmetry and correspondence: one of the most symmetrical pieces composed in this form is the first movement of Schubert's (Great) C major Symphony. Yet the careful patterning in no way prevents this movement from rising to dramatic climaxes or from maintaining an urgent, forward drive.

21. *Op. cit.*, pp. 83–84.

22. Another is the conduct of the debate, which will be examined in my next chapter.

23. Traditionally interpreted as a symbol of the 'two natures in one person' of Christ. But this interpretation has recently been challenged, and an entirely different one proposed, by Colin Hardie in *Centenary Essays on Dante by Members of the Oxford Dante Society* (Oxford, 1965), pp. 103–31.

CHAPTER THREE

1. M. P. Tilley, *Dictionary of the Proverbs in England of the Sixteenth and Seventeenth Centuries* (Michigan Univ., 1950), No. G. 393. See also F. P. Wilson, *The Proverbial Wisdom of Shakespeare* (*MHRA*, 1961), p. 18, where he cites *Faerie Queene*, I, x, 38.

2. *CT*, B.4130–31. Pertelote is also like the dreamer in *Pearl* in her inability to make distinctions. She dismisses all dreams as 'vanitees', empty of significance; whereas Chantecleer, although he is anxious to prove that his dream is prophetic, nevertheless shows his superior grasp of the subject by admitting a distinction (between the *somnium naturale* and the *somnium coeleste*):

> ' "... ther shul ye see
> Wher dremes be *somtyme – I say nat alle –*
> Warnynge of thynges that shul after falle." '
>
> (B.4320–22 – my italics)

An excellent example of a fictional debate in which the more enlightened character refutes his opponent's contentions through his ability to 'distinguish' occurs in *Piers Plowman*, B, iii, 229 ff., where Conscience demolishes the claims that Lady Meed had made for herself with his distinction between the 'two manere of medes'. The establishing of formal distinctions – especially when one 'authority' is being weighed against another – was an essential part of the scholastic method of argument. This can most readily be appreciated by glancing at the procedure which Aquinas adopts in answering any of the *quaestiones* that make up his *Summa Theologiae*.

3. On the use of legal phraseology in this stanza, see D. Everett and N. D. Hurnard, *M. AE.*, xvi, 9 ff.; see also E. G. Stanley (ed.), *The Owl and the Nightingale* (London and Edinburgh, 1960), p. 117, where he comments on a similar use of *inume* in l. 541 of that poem. In her book on *Pearl* (see Bibliographical Note, above, p. 129), Miss Kean has some interesting things to say about the use of legal terminology throughout the whole of the argument between the maiden and the dreamer (pp. 175 ff.).

4. Cf. *Piers Plowman*, B, viii, 28: 'seuene sithes the sadman on the day synneth'. See also the note on this line in W. W. Skeat (ed.), *The Vision of William Concerning Piers the Plowman. In Three Parallel Texts* (London, 1886), ii, p. 133.

PART TWO: INTRODUCTORY

1. A notable exception is Edwin Honig, *Dark Conceit: The Making of Allegory* (New York, 1966; first published 1959). Admittedly, Honig begins (p. 3) by referring to the distinction between allegory and symbolism, but the main argument of his book implies that its importance has been exaggerated (see esp. pp. 44 ff.). His study, however, has little bearing upon the problem of how to understand a medieval poem that involves allegory and symbolism. Much the same is true of another recent attempt to vindicate allegory as a literary mode: Angus Fletcher, *Allegory: The Theory of a Symbolic Mode* (Ithaca, New York, 1964).

CHAPTER FOUR

1. See C. G. Osgood, *Boccaccio on Poetry* (Princeton University Press, 1930; reprinted Indianapolis and New York, 1956).
2. See above, pp. 63; 65–66.
3. *ST*, I, i, 9, *ad primum*.
4. Ulrich of Strasbourg, *Summa de Bono*, Lib. i, ed. J. Daguillon (Paris, 1930), p. 52.
5. *ST*, I, i, 10.
6. *Ibid., ad tertium*.

K

7. *Ibid.* All quotations from the Latin text of the *Summa* are taken from the following ed.: *S. Thomae de Aquino Summa Theologiae*, 5 vols. (Ottawa, 1941), Tom. i.

8. *ST*, I, i, 10.

9. *Ibid.* The English translation is taken from: *The Summa Theologica of St. Thomas Aquinas*, Pt. 1, Qq. i–xxvi, tr. by Fathers of the English Dominican Province (London, 1921), p. 17.

10. For a succinct discussion of the difference, see Edgar De Bruyne, *L'Esthétique du Moyen Age* (Louvain, 1947), pp. 86–99. His three-volume work, *Études d'Esthétique Médiévale* (Bruges, 1946), contains a detailed historical and critical study of all kinds of medieval allegory (*passim*, but especially in vol. iii). The most thorough account of the allegorical interpretation of Scripture will be found in H. de Lubac, *Exégèse Médiévale* (Paris, 1959–64). See also Beryl Smalley, *The Study of the Bible in the Middle Ages* (Oxford, 1941).

11. *Confessions*, VIII, ix.

12. *Isaiah* liii.

13. See Appendix, above, p. 126, for a discussion of editorial punctuation of these stanzas.

14. An interesting detail of this passage is the way in which the refrain, depending upon the 'link-word' *Jerusalem*, plays upon the typological senses of that city. The poet plays upon the meanings of his 'link-word' in many sections of the poem, but he usually achieves this by means of *adminatio*. Here, in Group XIV, it is brought about by the use of the *sensus spiritualis*. In l. 817, where the maiden is speaking of the historical city of the New Testament, we read:

> ' "In Jerusalem, Jordan, and Galalye,
> Þer as baptysed þe goude Saynt Jon . . ." '

This comes at the beginning of the penultimate stanza of the group. At the end of the group's final stanza – which has been concerned with the anagogical sense of Jerusalem – the name occurs in conjunction with two other place-names. The new juxtaposition insists upon our understanding the name in its anagogical sense, as a synonym for Heaven:

> ' "And at þat syȝt vche douth con dare
> In helle, in erþe, and Jerusalem." ' (ll. 839–40)

15. As defined in *Convivio*, ii, 10; see above, p. 51.

16. See above, pp. 53-54.

17. Among the champions of this view in recent times are: P. Mandonnet, *Dante le Théologien* (Paris, 1935); E. R. Curtius, *European Literature &c.*, pp. 372–78.

18. Especially in his essay, 'Figura', in *Scenes from the Drama of European Literature* (New York, 1959), pp. 11–76. In this collection of papers by Auerbach it is translated by Ralph Manheim from the original German text in *Neue Dante-studien* (Istanbul, 1944), pp. 11–71. See also his chapter on 'Farinata and Cavalcante' in *Mimesis: The Representation of Reality in Western Literature* (trans. W. Trask; New York, 1957), pp. 151–77. The original German ed. was published at Berne in 1946.

19. *Dante the Philosopher* (trans. David Moore; London, 1948). The original ed. is *Dante et la Philosophie* (Paris, 1939). The book contains a brilliant refutation of Mandonnet's arguments.

20. *Ibid.*, 86–98.
21. See Charles S. Singleton, 'Dante's Allegory', *Speculum*, xxv, 78 ff. Cf. also above, p. 54.
22. Singleton, *art. cit.*
23. *Scenes from the Drama of European Literature*, p. 75.
24. See above, p. 53; also above, pp. 70, 81-84.
25. See below, Chapters 7 and 8.

CHAPTER FIVE

1. The distinction between tropes and figures was never very clearly or consistently defined. 'Figure' was the broader term that was sometimes used to include 'trope', so I shall use the term 'figure' to refer to either.
2. *Institutio Oratoria*, VIII, vi, 44.
3. *Isidori Hispanensis Episcopi Etymologiarum sive Originum Libri XX*, ed. W. M. Lindsay (Oxford, 1911), I, xxxvii, 22 ff.
4. *Vincentius Bellovacensis Speculum Maius*, 4 vols. (Vienna, 1591); 'Speculum Doctrinale', ii, 193.
5. For text in his *De Schematibus*, see C. F. von Halm, *Rhetores Latini Minores* (Leipzig, 1863), pp. 615 ff. A text of the relevant passage will also be found in *PL*, xc, 184–86.
6. Isidore defines the figure at *op. cit.*, II, xiii, as follows: 'Prosopopoeia est, cum inanimalium et persona et sermo fingitur, Cicero in Catilinam (i, 27): "Etenim si mecum patria mea, quae mihi vita mea multo est carior, loquetur, dicens . . . et cetera". Sic et montes et flumina vel arbores loquentes inducimus, personam imponentes rei quae non habet naturam loquendi.'
7. *Ed. cit.*, pp. xi–xii.
8. *The Allegory of Love* (corrected reprint; London, 1938), pp. 46–48.
9. *Vita Nuova*, xxv. See E. Moore (ed.), *Le Opere di Dante Alighieri* (Oxford, 1924), p. 223(a), ll. 60–71. Auerbach uses the term 'allegory' as a synonym for 'personification' (*Scenes from the Drama of European Literature*, p. 54). Similarly, Gilson's remarks (*op. cit.*, p. 73) about allegory in the *Roman de la Rose* show that he does not distinguish between the two figures.
10. *The Philosophy of Rhetoric* (London, 1936), Lectures v and vi, *passim*.
11. *De Augmentis Scientiarum*, II, xiii.
12. Halm (ed.), *Rhetores Latini Minores*, p. 616.
13. *Op. cit.*, I, xxxvii, 26.
14. Text from Edmond Faral, *Les Arts Poétiques du XIIᵉ et du XIIIᵉ Siècle* (Paris, 1924), p. 177 (§43).
15. *Ibid.*, §44.
16. *ST*, I, i, 9, *ad secundum*.
17. II, xliii; ed. E. Underhill (London, 1923), p. 443.
18. See the author's comment in B. Prologue, 208–9.
19. *ST*, I, i, 9, *resp.* See also Ulrich of Strasbourg, *Summa de Bono (ed. cit.)*, p. 52.
20. See above, p. 55.
21. See above, p. 53.
22. See above, p. 53.
23. Ed. Phyllis Hodgson (*EETS*, O.S. 218; London, 1944), pp. 112–13.
24. *Inferno*, ix, 61–63.

25. See above, p. 136, n. 23.
26. See above, pp. 53; 60; 80–84.
27. See above, pp. 60–61.
28. See above, p. 64.
29. See above, pp. 64–65.

CHAPTER SIX

1. On the significance of *luf-daungere* in this passage, see the article by W. R. J. arron in *A Medieval Miscellany Presented to Eugène Vinaver* (Manchester, 1965), pp. 1–18. After a careful survey of its use in O.Fr. and ME, Barron suggests that *daunger* in l. 250, as well as the compound in l. 11, should be rendered 'f ustration'.
2. *Ed. cit.*, p. 49.
3. In her book on *Pearl* (see Bibliographical Note, above, p. 129), Miss Kean (pp. 40 ff.) discusses the importance in the poet's argument of the notion of a contention between Reason and Will.
4. Miss Kean (*ibid.*, pp. 237 ff.) throws some light on the meaning of the terms *destyné, wyrd* and *fortune* in *Pearl*, not only by considering Boethius's use of corresponding terms, but also by examining the meanings that are given to them in the other poems in MS. Cotton Nero A x.
5. The possessive *þy* pulls *wyrde* away from the category of personification, but the fact that this *wyrde* is described as a thief exerts its pull in the opposite direction.
6. See *De Consolatione Philosophiae*, V, Prosa i (latter part).
7. At least, they are related according to *OED*. *MED* does not admit this etymology for *dongoun* (see under *dongoun* and *dong*).
8. See above, p. 63.
9. *Bref* may also convey the meaning 'small, trifling, insignificant': see *MED*, *bref* adj. 3(a). *MED* cites a line from the lyric in MS. Harley 2253 about the labourers in the vineyard: 'a peny that was so bref' (G. L. Brook, *The Harley Lyrics* – Manchester, 1948 – p. 43).
10. Professor J. A. W. Bennett has suggested to me that there may be an allusion here to *Matthew* vi, 19–20.
11. On the meaning of l. 341 see Gollancz's note (*ed. cit.*, p. 136). But see also the note on *Sir Gawain and the Green Knight*, l. 1296, in his ed. of that poem (*EETS*, O.S. 210; London, 1940), p. 114, which also discusses the use of *blesse* in *Pearl*.
12. The author can hardly have been aware of the etymology of *ʒemen*. A further example of his use of *expolitio* is seen in his expansion of the Vulgate's 'Circa undecimam' into:

    ' "At the date of daye of euensonge,
      On oure byfore þe sonne go doun . . ." '   (ll. 529–30)

But he is not alone in using *euensonge* in this context: see the verse paraphrase of this parable in MS. Harley 2253 (Brook, *ed. cit.*, p. 42), l. 13.
13. See above, p. 93.
14. See above, pp. 95–97.
15. When considering the meaning of 'homly', we should remember the use of 'patria' by patristic and other writers to refer to Paradise, from which we are exiled and imprisoned in 'þys doel-doungoun' (l. 1187).

16. *PMLA*, xix, 154–215.
17. Sister Mary Madeleva, *Pearl: A Study in Spiritual Dryness* (New York, 1925).
18. See Bibliographical Note, above, p. 129.
19. *Ed. cit.*, pp. xi ff.
20. *Ibid.*, p. xii.
21. See above, p. 64.
22. For an interesting discussion of the poet's procedure in this passage, see the article by C. A. Luttrell listed in Bibliographical Note, above, p. 129.
23. The following paragraphs reproduce – with some modifications – part of my article in *RES* (N.S.), viii, 12–21; esp. pp. 14–15.
24. See *ibid.*, p. 14, and Schofield, *PMLA*, xxiv, 600–6.
25. On the syntax of these lines, see Gordon, *ed. cit.*, p. 45. Gordon remarks that they 'are probably not an apostrophe'. A comparison with the opening lines of the Lapidary verses confirms this view.
26. But not necessarily so, as Gordon has pointed out, *ed. cit.*, p. 45.
27. *RES* (N.S.), viii, 14, n. 2.
28. See ll. 257–64, and the whole of the following stanza.
29. See above, p. 30, n. 14. Also *art. cit.*, *passim*.
30. There is something to be said for Luttrell's suggestion (p. 71 of the critical anthology ed. by Blanch – see Bibliographical Note, above, p. 128) that *schyneʒ* (l. 28) should be emended to *schyne* (infinitive, dependent like *sprede* on *mot*) with the implication that spices, flowers and fruit *ought* to spring from the buried pearl. But I prefer to retain the MS. reading and assume that the spices have in fact sprung from the pearl. Whichever reading is adopted, it makes little difference to my interpretation of the passage.
31. *Ed. cit.*, p. 48.
32. Gollancz (*ed. cit.*, p. 118) compares *Hamlet*, V, ii:

> 'And from her fair and unpolluted flesh
> May violets spring.'

Osgood remarks (*ed. cit.*, p. 55) that a virgin is called 'swetture þan eny spis' in Thomas of Hales, 'A Love Ron' (l. 168), and Gordon observes (*ed. cit.*, p. 48) that 'the lady Joan' (*sic* – surely he means 'the lady Annot') is compared to a series of spices in the lyric 'Annot and Johon' in MS. Harley 2253. It should be added that three of the spices specified in *Pearl* are included in this series:

> 'Ase *gromyl* in greue grene is þe grone
> ase quibibe ant comyn cud is in crone,
> cud comyn in court, canel in cofre,
> wiþ *gyngyure* ant sedewale ant þe *gylofre*.'

(My italics – text from Brook, *ed. cit.*, p. 32, ll. 37–40.) It should also be noticed that in the first stanza of this lyric the lady is compared to a series of precious stones, including the 'margarite' (*ed. cit.*, p. 31, l. 9). Another interesting point is that this opening stanza employs two Lapidary formulas: 'ase gernet in golde' (l. 4); 'he is coral ycud wiþ cayser and knyht' (l. 7).
33. A particularly striking example intrudes itself into a passage where Hugh of St. Victor purports to be discussing the variety of colours among flowers: *PL*, clxxvi, 821.
34. See above, pp. 17–18.

35. See C. L. Wrenn, 'On Re-reading Spenser's *The Shepheardes Calender*', *Essays and Studies by Members of the English Association*, xxix, 30 ff.; see esp. pp. 31–32. The vision is remedial, not only because it assures the mourner of the maiden's survival, but because it sets him on the path to his own salvation. His spiritual renewal is therefore one of the 'fruits' of her death.

36. Cf. St. Augustine's similar use of the image in a consolatory topic, cited above, p. 18.

37. See Osgood, *ed. cit.*, p. xvi, n. 5.

38. *Ed. cit.*, p. 47.

39. As long ago as 1950 Professor G. V. Smithers drew my attention to this way of interpreting ll. 39–40. On the traditional 'occupations of the months', see R. Tuve, *Seasons and Months in Middle English Poetry* (Paris, 1933); Emile Mâle, *L'Art Religieux du XIIIIe Siècle en France* (Paris, 1925), pp. 63–75.

40. For ed. from which text is taken, see below, p. 143, n. 9.

41. Brook, *ed. cit.*, p. 40.

42. *MED* – under *grain* n. 3(b) – gives only this instance and one from *The Prioress's Tale* as examples of the sense 'precious stone . . . gem'.

43. *Ed. cit.*, p. 120.

44. *MLN*, lxiv, 83–84.

45. Tom. ii (Paris, 1886), p. 740; under *grémil*.

46. Under *gremil* it gives: 'the herb *gromill*; *grummell*; *graymill*; *peare-plant* [*sic*]'.

47. *Pace* R. J. Blanch (see Bibliographical Note, above, p. 128), who shows that references to the various virtues, concepts and doctrines that are associated in the lapidaries with each of these gems occur at various points in the poem. But the association plays no part in the poem's 'plot': the poet makes no cross-references – either explicitly or implicitly – between a particular doctrine or virtue and a particular gem.

48. See Gordon, *ed. cit.*, p. xxx.

49. Especially descriptions of the *locus amoenus* and of the Earthly Paradise. For an account of these traditions, see: E. R. Curtius, *European Lit. &c.*, Chapter x; J. A. W. Bennett, *The Parlement of Foules: An Interpretation* (Oxford, 1957), Chapter ii *passim*, but esp. p. 71, n. 1 (for further references) and p. 78.

50. See above, p. 35.

51. See Gordon, *ed. cit.*, pp. xxvii–xxix. For further associations of ladies with pearls, see above, p. 87 and p. 141, n. 32. For the use in medieval art of pearls as symbols of the virtuous inhabitants of Heaven, see above, p. 84. With the sentiment expressed in ll. 1211–12, cf. *Purity*, l. 1116: '& pure þe with penaunce tyl þou a perle worþe'. Cf. also the simile in *Sir Gawain and the Green Knight* ll. 2364–65.

52. A similar principle is illustrated in the parable of the treasure hidden in the field, which immediately precedes that of the pearl of great price in *Matthew* xiii, 44. But the image of the pearl was obviously much more adaptable for the poet's peculiar combination of significances.

53. See above, p. 16.

54. Professor J. A. W. Bennett has reminded me of a passage in another fourteenth-century English poem where the parable of the pearl of great price is associated with the notion of the *summum bonum*; namely, *Piers Plowman*, C, vi, 92–101.

55. See above, pp. 74–75.

56. *JEGP*, liv, 341–42.
57. See above, p. 83. See also p. 19.
58. *Luke* xvii, 21. An alternative translation is 'among you'. The meaning of the preposition in the Vulgate is ambiguous: '... regnum Dei intra vos est'. For the idea that men (specifically, 'the peacemakers') may in themselves become a Kingdom of God, see Augustine, *De Sermone Domini in Monte*, I, ii, 9 (*PL*, xxxix, 1233).
59. See above, pp. 19-21.
60. See above, p. 61.
61. See above, pp. 34-35.
62. See above, p. 61. See also pp. 19-21
63. Text from *The Works of George Herbert*, ed. F. E. Hutchinson (Oxford, 1941), p. 88.

PART THREE: INTRODUCTORY

1. *Ed. cit.*, p. xxv, n. 3; cf. *De Civitate Dei*, xxii, 14 and 15. Dante's assumption (*Paradiso*, xxxii, 46–47) that children retain their childish faces and voices in Heaven is contrary to the normal medieval opinion.
2. *Ed. cit.*, 63–64; n. on l. 197.
3. '*The Pearl*: An Interpretation of the Middle English Poem', *Studies in English*, iv (Charles University, Prague, 1933) – esp. pp. 20–24. Reprinted in Blanch, *op. cit.* (see Bibliographical Note, above, p. 128); esp. pp. 24 ff.
4. All references to the Sarum Missal and Breviary are to the following edd.: *The Sarum Missal*, ed. J. Wickham Legg (Oxford, 1916); F. Proctor and C. Wordsworth, *Breviarium ad Usum Insignis Ecclesiae Sarum* (Cambridge, 1879–86), 3 vols.
5. I give references to book, chapter and paragraph. The edition from which I quote is that published at Naples in 1859. Many helpful annotations will be found in the French translation of this work: *Rational ou Manuel des Divins Offices de Guillaume Durand*, ed. Charles Barthélemy (Paris, 1854), 5 vols. An English trans. of Book I appears in J. M. Neale and B. Webb, *The Symbolism of Churches and Church Ornaments* (Leeds, 1843), and of Book III in T. H. Passmore, *The Sacred Vestments* (London, 1899).
6. Durandus acknowledges the fact that his work is a compilation from other sources (VIII, xiv). For a list of some of the authors whom he consulted, see Barthélemy, *ed. cit.*, I, xxv. In V, 467–79, he gives a list of the principal liturgical commentators arranged chronologically.
7. Honorius's works are edited in *PL*, clxxii.
8. It is printed in the edition of Durandus's *Rationale* (Naples, 1859) mentioned above. A text of Belethus's *Rationale* will also be found in *PL*, ccii.
9. Text from the following edition: 'Bartholomaeus de proprietatibus rerum .. translated from latin into our vulgaire langage by John of Trevisa. Londoni in aedibus Thomae Bertheleti [1535]'.

CHAPTER SEVEN

1. *MLN*, xlii, 113–16.
2. *CT*, B.1769–75.
3. *Ibid.*, B.1817.

4. Cf. *CT*, B. 1709.

5. *Sarum Breviary, ed. cit.*, I, ccxlii. For Wyclif's opinion that musical settings – among other features of the Salisbury ritual – distract attention from the *sentence*, see his treatise 'Of Feigned Contemplative Life' in *The English Works of Wyclif*, ed. F. D. Matthew (*EETS*, O.S., 74), pp. 187–96.

6. On the Boy Bishop see (apart from primary sources mentioned in subsequent notes): E. K. Chambers, *The Medieval Stage* (Oxford, 1903), i, 336–71; Daniel Rock, *The Church of Our Fathers*, new edn. by G. W. Hart and W. H. Frere (London, 1904), iv, 250–56; J. M. J. Fletcher, *The Boy Bishop at Salisbury and Elsewhere* (Salisbury, 1921); W. C. Meller, *The Boy Bishop* (London, 1923). Meller does little more than Fletcher.

7. See Durandus of Mende, *Rationale*, VII, xlii, 15, as well as secondary sources mentioned in preceding note.

8. *Sarum Breviary, ed. cit.*, I, ccxxix.

9. See Meller, *op. cit.*, p. 13.

10. Text is given in *Camden Miscellany*, VII (Publications of the Camden Society, N.S., No. xiv, 1875), pp. 14 ff.; see Fletcher, *op. cit.*, p. 18; Meller, *op. cit.*, p. 14.

11. Meller, *op. cit.*, pp. 12–13.

12. C. Wordsworth, *Ceremonies and Processions of the Cathedral Church of Salisbury* (Cambridge, 1901), p. 52.

13. Lines 205-7.

14. Line 211.

15. The available evidence suggests that these ceremonies were widespread throughout England during the fourteenth century: see Fletcher, *op. cit.*, pp. 9–10; Meller, *op. cit.*, pp. 10–11.

16. *Medieval Stage*, ii, 148; *English Literature at the Close of the Middle Ages* (Oxford, 1945), pp. 7–9.

17. *The Drama of the Medieval Church* (Oxford, 1933), ii, 102–24.

18. *Ibid.*, p. 105.

19. *Ibid.*, pp. 110–13. Text also given in T. Wright, *Early Mysteries and Other Latin Poems of the Twelfth and Thirteenth Centuries* (London, 1838), pp. 29–31; E. du Méril, *Origines Latines Du Théâtre Moderne* (Paris, 1849), pp. 175–79.

20. The Innocents are also associated with the procession of *Revelation* xiv in hymns, such as that by Bede (*Anal. Hymnica*, L, p. 102 and see XLII, p. 225); see also the carol by John Audelay, mentioned by Gordon, *ed. cit.*, p. xxv, n. 2. Gordon also refers to the Towneley play of Herod.

21. See above, p. 104.

22. On baptism by martyrdom, cf. *Piers Plowman*, B. xii, 282–83:

> 'For there is fullyng of fonte . and fullyng in blode-shedynge,
> And thorugh fuire is fullyng . and that is ferme bileue.'

(W. W. Skeat, *The Vision of William Concerning Piers the Plowman*. In Three Parallel Texts – London, 1886 – i, 382.)

23. Lines 645–48.

24. *Mirk's Festial*, ed. T. Erbe, I (*EETS*, E.S., 96), p. 35.

25. They do not appear in the modern Roman Breviary; neither are they included in the medieval York Breviary: see *Breviarium ad Usum Insignis Ecclesiae Eboracensis*, i (Surtees Society, lxxi (1880; 1879 on spine), coll. 112–20). The

three final *lectiones* (which do not, in fact, concern us here) are, like the corresponding ones in *Sarum*, taken from Bede – but they are not identical with them.

26. *Sarum Breviary, ed. cit.*, I, ccxxxiv. The *lectio* is concerned with the antiphon: 'quare non defendis . . .'

27. *Ibid.* col. ccxxxv (by Severianus).

28. Psalm xv in *A.V.*

29. *Sarum Breviary, ed. cit.*, I ccxxxvi.

30. Moreover, it may also provide a possible source for an important aspect of the poem's didactic *sentence*. In addition to evidence already mentioned, we may observe an annotation by Barthélemy (see above, p. 143, n. 5) on a passage in which Durandus discusses the liturgy for Holy Innocents' Day. He calls attention to a homily for the Feast by Pope St. Leo the Great [i.e. Leo I] (Barthélemy, *ed. cit.*, v, 342–45). The homily exhorts its audience to become as children and is concerned with the spiritual renewal of life; it urges a return to infancy, not in ignorance, but in harmlessness.

CHAPTER EIGHT

1. Text from Edmond Faral, *Les Arts Poétiques du XIIe et du XIIIe Siècle* (Paris, 1924), p. 120. This is Matthew's adaptation, for purposes of the *descriptio*, of Horace's precept about consistency of characterization (De Arte Poetica, II, 120 ff.).

2. *PL*, clxxii, 673.

3. *Ibid.*, col. 616.

4. See P. Guéranger, *The Liturgical Year*: the vol. entitled 'Passiontide and Holy Week' in the trans. by L. Shepherd (Dublin, 1870), pp. 614–19.

5. For the form of baptism observed in medieval England, see W. Maskell, *Monumenta Ritualia Ecclesiae Anglicanae* (London, 1846), i, 22-36. Maskell reproduces the text of the Sarum rite, but in footnotes he observes discrepancies between it and the other medieval English rites.

6. *Rationale*, cap. cx (*PL*, ccii, 114).

7. See Durandus, *op. cit.*, VI, lxxxiii, 17.

8. *Ibid.*, 15.

9. *Ibid.*

10. See above, p. 121.

11. Lines 603-4.

12. See above, p. 101.

13. See Honorius as quoted above, p. 115 and n. 3.

14. See above, p. 114 and n. 2. So also Durandus: '. . . quia ipse est *membrum* Christi, qui est rex et sacerdos' (see above, p. 116 and n. 8).

15. *Ed. cit.*, p. 54.

16. *Op. cit.*, VI, lxxxiii, 16, where he is discussing the significance of the chrisom. See also *ibid.*, III, xviii, 2. This chapter is concerned with the various uses of the four liturgical colours.

17. *Ibid.*, III, iii, 5. The opening of the quotation from *Ephesians* is a corruption of *Ephesians* iv, 22: 'Deponere vos secundum pristinam conversationem veterem hominem . . .' Cf. *Colossians* iii, 9 and 10.

18. The application of the four allegorical 'senses' to the liturgical text as well as to the vestments and ecclesiastical ornaments is a common feature of the liturgical commentaries. See Durandus, *op. cit.*, I, *Proemium*, 6–12.

19. *PL*, clxxii, 749.

20. *Op. cit.*, VI, lxxxi, 13.

21. *Sarum Breviary, ed. cit.*, I, dcccxviii–dcccxxii.

22. But usually, no doubt, there were infants to be baptized on that day. The Sarum Missal makes provision for baptism in the course of the Holy Saturday ceremonies, giving instructions for the putting on of the chrisom (*ed. cit.*, p. 131).

23. *Sarum Missal, ed. cit.*, p. 144.

CHAPTER NINE

1. *Matthew* xx, 1–16.

2. Lines 497 ff.

3. C. F. Brown, 'The Author of *The Pearl* Considered in the Light of his Theological Opinions', *PMLA*, xix, 115–53.

4. See Bibliographical Note, above, p. 130.

5. Line 530.

6. Line 582.

7. 'The "Heresy" of *The Pearl*', *MLN*, lxv, 152–55.

8. *PL*, clxv, 237.

9. See ll. 484–85.

10. Lines 585–86.

11. Cf. ll. 477–78.

12. *PL*, clxxii, 858.

13. *Ibid.*, my italics.

14. *Ed. cit.*, p. 74.

15. *Patience*, ll. 9–10.

16. The sermon also contains the famous allegorization of the story of Ulysses and the Sirens, which is discussed by H. O. Taylor, *The Mediaeval Mind* (fourth ed. reprinted, Cambridge, Mass., 1959), ii, 83–85.

Index